DATE DUE

THE MEANING AND TEACHING
OF MUSIC

THE MEANING AND TEACHING OF MUSIC

by Will Earhart

WITMARK EDUCATIONAL PUBLICATIONS
DEPARTMENT OF M. WITMARK & SONS
NEW YORK

Printed in the United States of America by
J. J. LITTLE & IVES COMPANY, NEW YORK

TO MY WIFE

FOREWORD

During many years of teaching the author of this book has been trying to sum up his thoughts on the nature of music, the ways of teaching it, and its possible values. Increasingly during the two decades ending in 1929 he was disturbed by the fact that educators and people generally, although predisposed in sentiment to concede the values of music, were adherents to lines of thought and action which did not in the least supply grounds for their favorable predisposition. Nor could the many current forms of teaching music, and the various current conceptions of its nature, be separated from this problem of its values. Philosophy, aesthetics, psychology, and the practice of teaching, appeared to be inseparably interwoven and to constitute one problem, the component parts of which would have to agree.

This book is the result, then, of that which began as a personal inquiry. It is obviously not a work on philosophy, aesthetics, or psychology; but it is the work of a teacher who sought in those three fields some guidance that would enable him to teach better and with clearer and wider vision.

Specifically, the work has been brought to a head in the last two years. Before that, many of the constituent thoughts had been incorporated in courses of lectures given to teachers of music in summer sessions of various American colleges, had been put forward as principles underlying departmental work in a city school system, and occasionally had become subjects for articles in magazines, or for papers read before musical and educational groups. Those numerous reworkings brought greater clarity to the parts and greater coherence to the whole; although it must be admitted that at the time they were formulated their organization into a book was not even remotely contemplated. In the fall of 1932, however, the author began to teach a graduate course in Carnegie Institute of Technology, Pittsburgh; and this course was repeated in 1933-34. The ample time provided gave opportunity for a more complete assembling and organization of the factors than had ever before been possible, and also gradually revealed the desirability of writing down essentials of the course. For existing literature provided text materials, when at all, only in pages scattered through a wide range of volumes; and efforts of students to collect the essentials of the course made it difficult for them to do the large amount of enriching reading that was desired. A core text such as this, that might serve as a point of departure, was therefore needed.

The author feels grateful for the type of students he had in his classes during the two years referred to. They were very alert and responsive. Most of them were fellow-teachers; and all became fellow-students with him. Their mental activity, more than any other factor, made the course appear significant and valuable, and encouraged the author in his attempt to write it for the use of others like them.

Although the work is largely abstract, the author hopes it will be found to have practical bearings. His own interest in it is wholly practical; for every part of it has been used to inform and direct the teaching of music in a city school system, and not in a vague way, but in explicit application to many details of method and practice. Primarily, however, it is not for the neophyte who has yet to attain the beginnings of a technique of teaching, but is rather for those who, already able to teach, would scrutinize again their principles of teaching and reflect anew upon the nature and possible values of their work.

Pittsburgh, Pa.

January 15, 1935.

CONTENTS

PART FOUR. *Specific Forms of Practice*

Appendix

THE MEANING AND TEACHING
OF MUSIC

THE PHILOSOPHICAL BASIS

CHAPTER ONE

Tendencies in Philosophy

Origins of modern thought

The last hundred years or more have witnessed a gradual but stupendous change in western civilization, the chief characteristics of which are due to the mastery of natural forces by man through his continued progress in the physical sciences. The mental turn which provided the basis for this development arose in late Renaissance times. Galileo studied the physical universe and made discoveries that, in the words of Bergson,[1] "revealed the possibility of bringing down some astronomical and physical problems to those of mechanics." Contemporary with him, and imbued with a turn of thought which impelled them along similar paths, were Kepler, Descartes, and Bacon. The latter gave the new movement powerful impetus by formulating and upholding its philosophy and urging its wide application. The inductive method, reliance upon observation and experiment, devotion to and faith in scientific investigation, were outlined by him as a system which alone was appropriate for man to follow in finding a way of life in the universe about

---

[1] *Mind-Energy:* Henri Bergson.

I

him. All inquiry was to be in "the dry light of reason."
The brilliant progress in the sciences in the centuries that
followed, and their contribution to man's material welfare,
finally, it would seem, brought this Baconian view of man's
nature and normal mental action into almost universal
acceptance.

Extension of the new outlook

For a time, however, the new rationalistic thought applied itself only to the inorganic universe. Haldane [1] de-
scribes with precision the situation at that point when he
says: "But until more recent times the phenomena of life
and of conscious behavior were usually excluded from the
scope of this interpretation, so that traditional science could
not be called materialistic. Roughly speaking, it left us with
the conception of a physical world and a spiritual world
existing side by side with it." But throughout the centuries
that elapsed after Galileo and his contemporaries unfolded
a new picture of the universe, their modes of thought
gained greater currency and were applied to an ever-
widening range of phenomena. Gradually the assumption
arose that not only were the heavenly bodies a gigantic
mechanism, and the earth a clock-work of physical and
chemical actions, but that living organisms also might be
fully explained in precisely similar terms. As Bergson [2] states
this projection of the Galilean point of view: "Thence arose

[1] *Materialism:* J. S. Haldane.
[2] *Mind-Energy:* Henri Bergson.

the idea that the whole universe, *organic* and inorganic, might be an immense machine, governed by mathematical laws." (The italics are mine.) And Haldane [1] alludes to the same departure as, "the belief that the external universe can be interpreted, without residue, in terms of physical, including chemical, conceptions."

Phenomena as external

The *external* universe: it is necessary that we ask what is included and what excluded under that term. Characteristically it is applied to matter that occupies space. Heavenly bodies, mountains and sands, the objects that compose a landscape that we may be observing, come easily within its purview. But plants, animals, persons, even my friend, also are externalized in space. Increasingly, however, as we run through these latter terms do we find it difficult to maintain our original concept of the external as detached physical bodies occupying space. Only by a violent effort am I able to imagine myself regarding my friend in that light: and if I succeed in so regarding him I find that this new and unnatural regard is attained, not by adding something to my normal cognizance of him, but by subtracting much. That which is subtracted is his meaning, his value, all that makes him my friend; and in getting rid of these I must similarly strip from my own way of regarding him any tendency to seek meanings or values or aught else than is present to my senses and to that part of my

[1] J. S. Haldane: *op. cit.*

mind which weighs and appraises physical phenomena reported by the senses. In short I must regard him as so much matter, if not inert then as animated only, as are air or water, by physical forces. So long as I thus limit my regard of him, I am prepared to examine him scientifically, by means of scales, the microscope, the thermometer, chemical tests, and other instrumentalities of precision and of exact, quantitative knowledge. I am also prepared to reason on, and draw conclusions with respect to his physical future; but I am not prepared to greet him as my friend, or to discuss with him his moral, ethical, or aesthetic preferences and problems. His externality is therefore not the essential principle of his being, but is rather one peculiar aspect of his being, and is a salient aspect only when discerned from a special and limited point of view maintained within myself.

What the external view contributes

So long as the special and limited point of view, or "method of knowing," as Dewey [1] terms it, is understood to *be* special and limited, much good and little evil can come of it. It is the point of view characteristic of and appropriate to the physical sciences, or the "sciences of matter" as Bergson would say, and our dealings with matter and our consequent present material well-being flow almost wholly from its promptings. Unfortunately this "method of knowing," has come to be regarded by many as the only method by which truth can be apprehended, and the reali-

[1] *Reconstruction in Philosophy:* John Dewey.

ties it discovers have come to be accepted as the only and sufficient Reality. On this point, as well as on the benefits conferred by science, Haldane [1] says: "We have invented the various methods of science for our own practical purposes. They make it more easy to see into the future and past and to plan our behaviour in detail.—Let us, therefore, make all the use we can of the physical conception of our universe. It embodies a view, though only *a very partial view, of actual reality,* and is a most useful conception for many practical purposes. In this sense, but *in this sense alone,* it represents reality. It would be madness to discard it because its uses are only limited." (The italics are mine.) In similar vein Bergson,[2] discussing "mathematical proof—that creation of Greek genius," lauds "the precision, the exactness, the anxiety for proof, the habit of distinguishing between what is simply possible or probable and what is certain;" and he continues: "The habit of bringing to the study of concrete reality the same requirements of precision, of exactness, of certitude, which are characteristic of the mathematical mind is, therefore, a habit we owe to the sciences of matter and that we should not have had without them."

Rational powers

In our paragraph, "Phenomena as external," we implied that the mechanistic interpretation derived from the testimony of our senses, and engaged only the rational in-

---

[1] *Materialism:* J. S. Haldane.
[2] *Mind-Energy:* Henri Bergson.

tellect. The point needs explication; and that will be effected most readily, perhaps, by explaining a doctrine advanced by Bergson.

Bergson [1] maintains, then, that the rational intellect is formed on matter and its purpose is the manipulation of matter. In more explicit statement this means, first, that biologically our sense organs are believed to have been developed as responses to the play of physical forces upon formative material. They and that which they see and hear and otherwise apprehend are in union, are complementary, are two poles of one transaction. Upon such sensory testimony is based all of our exact knowledge of, and our forms of action upon, the physical world about us. Our rational intellect is therefore concerned with the knowledge gained through the senses, and with preparation for action based upon this knowledge. The rational intellect thus deals with a physical universe, and characteristically with the inorganic, or at least with the non-human; and it conceives this universe as operated under precise and unvarying laws. Its rejection of the organic, the living, the conscious, is due to the fact that in those fields are factors not directly known to the senses, factors that are not subject to investigation that can be reported in exact mathematical terms, and that display a freedom and a creative quality (as in the unprevised thought of human beings) that remove them from the reach of such confident predictions as can readily be made in the case of phenomena that are subject to physical laws.

[1] *Creative Evolution:* Henri Bergson.

Characteristics of Modern Thought

In the light of the foregoing discussion, modern thought, in a characteristic phase, appears as founded upon a belief that the external universe should be externally (or objectively or impersonally) regarded; that so regarded, as reported to the senses alone, we are bound to conceive it as Reality itself; that this physical reality operates under unvarying, physical laws; and that consequently the secrets of its operations can be discovered and reduced to rules, and their future outcomes can be forecast. As corresponding to the various phases of this intellectual system we can see, too, the significance of certain words and terms, some of which have been used and others of which may be useful later, such as objectivism, rationalism, and rationalistic; realism; mechanism, "mechanistic explanation," and "physico-realism"; and determinism. We can see, further, that this "method of knowing," although it by no means embraces the full field of thought of scientists themselves, as individuals, yet provides the materials and methods characteristic of the sciences they follow. And if we trace still further the influence of this rationalistic mode of intellection upon individuals and society, we shall gain an outlook upon the modern economic and social state that will be of considerable value to our inquiry.

Chapter Two

An Industrial Society as Related to Modern Thought

Materials and Meanings

Our physical senses acting alone report only physical conditions. The retina, as a physical organ, registers no more than does a photographic plate, and a landscape laid thereon, so far as physical science can regard it, holds no more meaning than the same landscape holds for the camera in which it is registered. Physical science need not deny that man contributes to such an optical registration more than is contributed by a camera; but physical science can easily—and if it remains pure science, indeed, it must—overlook or disregard that fact. As in the illustrative case of "my friend," it finds itself without the equipment and methods by which to do more than investigate the physically discernible. This is not to say that it can not grasp absent physical phenomena and predict future ones. By discovery of laws operative in the present, it can extend itself to the physically removed. In the end, however, immediate presence is necessary to it: that is to say, its ultimate proof will be found in the existence at some time, at some place, in some quantity, and in some condition, of a matter directly discernible to the physical senses. Astronomical observation, for instance, must verify or fail to verify Einstein's theory.

But the physical senses, and the rational intellect that studies the materials, conditions, and movements which they report, are in themselves without knowledge of meanings, of values, of ends. These are subjective contributions. As such they are open to suspicion on the part of the scientist; but for human life those same subjective responses, such as might arise from viewing a landscape, form the very essence of the experience. The mere physical fact that there *was an experience,* however minutely the physical nature of that experience be investigated and defined, is, from this point of view, meaningless. Only after the values have been predicated, indeed, can the physical sciences cooperate with humanity in the realm of ends. If the landscape contains a malarial swamp, the physicist can drain it and exterminate the pestilential mosquitoes; if its fields are sterile, he can analyze the soil and direct its fertilization. On the other hand, if he is an army engineer, he can quite as readily make the swamp more impassable and the terrain more inimical to human life.

It should be observed in passing, however, that in any case he *hypothecates ends* that are not implicit in the landscape as external, or in the materials and physical forces he deals with, but that reside solely in the breast of some human being. Desire for health, for food, or for destruction of an enemy, were the prompting motives in the case just assumed. These desires, it is true, all look toward physical well-being or toward material ends, and as such enter readily into the purview of science, and constitute the sort of ends that science can best serve. Nevertheless, the desires themselves are not physical, at last in this sense, that they are not physically present in the materials observed. This point will be clearer if we use another illustration. Let us suppose that the landscape, instead of being found unhealthful, had been judged to be unbeautiful, or less than perfect in its beauty. In this case the scientist would not be quite so ready to undertake material procedures. His difficulty would lie in the fact that the efficiency of his results could not be measured in exact, physical terms. Indeed, in so far as he remained a scientist, he could not pronounce the landscape either beautiful or unbeautiful; and were it even his own estate, and were a preliminary aesthetic judgment on his part conceded (but not explained), he could not proceed wholly as a scientist, because no material transformation he might effect could be scientifically proven to have produced beauty measurable in precise, quanitative terms.

Results versus Ends

The conclusion toward which we have been tending is that science can be efficient in producing material results, that are measurable in material terms, but that within itself it does not discern meanings or ends in the materials spread before it, and does not, therefore, hold the capacity to plan a program of ends. It will, nevertheless, because all action is inescapably based on an assumption of attainment of desirable ends, proceed toward *some* ends; and since certain immediate and practical ends are obviously desirable, at least superficially, and since such ends best adapt to its service, it will, all unconscious of its inconsistency, take them for granted and serve them; and a society comparatively fixed on material progress will follow. James Mackaye, in his book, *The Economy of Happiness,* puts much this same thought in different words when he says: "As science first encroaches upon intuitionism from the material side, its effect upon nations emerging from mediaevalism is to promote an industrial development out of proportion to their moral development. . . . Thus have arisen the great commercial nations of modern times—all hands and no head—with great capacity for doing things, but without capacity to distinguish what things are useful to do. . . . They use common sense as a guide to proximate ends, but intuition as a guide to ultimate ends." Without subscribing to one implication that possibly resides in the statement, to the effect that common sense (if by this is meant inductive reasoning) can lead us to ultimate ends, we can still accept the given description as accurate.

Moral Guidance and Efficiency

Had we sought from the proper sources wisdom as to what it is worth while to do we might readily have found it. In that case we should have been able to place science more surely in the service of the highest in man—which has been the dream of all the best of men, scientists and seers alike—instead of placing it, as has been done, indiscriminately in the service of all man's desires and passions, high and low alike. Never, it is true, could it have been restrained wholly, by any principle within itself, to the service of either good causes or bad, for in itself it generates no motives. These must be given; and being given, science then assumes its task, which is to know physical forces—not motives—and, perhaps, shape them toward definite and materially useful ends. By such movement it produces, let us say, the automobile. Useful and highly desirable ends were doubtless assumed as consequent upon its production, and in large degree these have been attained. Nevertheless, we can not be blind to the fact that the automobile aids the gangster and murderer as efficiently as it speeds the rescuer on some errand of mercy. And ever there is the danger pointed out by Mr. Mackaye, that, lacking motives but acquiring techniques, the technology based on science may spend far too much time and energy on the production of that which, if not evil, is at least trivial and futile.

Motives, then, since they do not lie on the face of the physical world nor lurk between its atoms, must be sought elsewhere. They would have been sought and would have been carefully considered had not the sources of knowledge other than those open to science been regarded with distrust, as "subjective." But the inductive "method of knowing" alone was given credence, and authority was attached only to its findings. What it could not discover was assumed, it would almost appear, to be non-existent, and what it could not accomplish was considered, one might think, as lying outside the pale of desirable achievement. In a word, the world has looked to science and its mode of thought to lead in realms in which it can appropriately only follow and serve. The expectation of Francis Bacon and of many of his modern followers is thus doomed to disappointment. Pondering on external facts will not guide us in a world of human desires and spiritual ends.

Homo faber

The effects of entrusting to the rational intellect problems that can be solved only by subjective testimony that appears at its highest in the clear vision and implicit understanding of great leaders and prophetic seers have become marked throughout our social organization. Restrained, by the very terms which give it its authority, to dealings with a physically operated universe, science characteristically first lays hold on man in his physical aspects, and, following that, as a unit of physical powers that is susceptible, as are all the physical forces it deals with, of control toward the production of concrete ends. That view of man is not new. It is always present in measure in man's consciousness of his own powers and of certain possibilities in his social unit. It has been adopted in military affairs ever since the first armies of ancient rulers were deployed upon the field; and the pyramids of Egypt were builded by means of it.

Nevertheless, the ancient view was not identical with that which now obtains. Regimentation of man's powers was of old regarded either as a temporary expedient for the many, as when men combined to wage a war, or as a permanent lot for a slave class or a proletariat, the members of which were frankly regarded as less than "free" men because of their status as units of efficient action. But such an outlook implied, by its very omissions, the existence of other beliefs about the nature and modes of functioning appropriate to man. Thus the view was resorted to only at critical junctures or in application to certain limited classes. It remained for a later generation to extend the rationalistic conception, in practice if not in theory, to mankind as a whole, and to organize society on principle as a mechanism for the production of specific results. Such shaping of natural forces, under the direction of rational powers, to the attainment of definite objectives, was the basis of the once much discussed German *Kultur*. It gave Germany her pre-war efficiency, alike in industry and in her military establishment. Such, also, is the basis upon which Soviet government is now striving to erect a mechanistic civilization that in material accomplishments shall surpass any yet known. To succeed in such a project requires only that humanity be regimented in terms of its capacities for material production, or, in other words, shall be regarded as a mobile mechanism. In such an enterprise in human engineering Russia is not singular: she has merely been logically thorough-going in her application of principles that originated elsewhere.

Humanity and Industrial Man

The effect of the mechanistic conception upon society is thus most quickly apparent in the industrial field. The

far quests of man's spirit may not be reached by its operations, but his physical well-being and material advantage
appear thereby to be guaranteed. In pursuit of such assur-
ance he bends his rational intellect upon the material world,
endlessly transports and transforms matter by physical and
chemical operations, and utilizes natural forces to his material welfare. In order to heighten his efficiency he invents
tools and machines that increasingly absorb him into themselves as a detail of themselves; and he operates these in
large industrial plants that tend to give him an artificial
environment. A tendency appears to forget, at times, man's
aspect as an individual human being, in preoccupation with
his aspect as a "hand," a workman, an employee. Moreover,
since production entails employment, wages, and profits,
and since wise ends are outside the purview of the rational
and efficient plan, there is constant danger that production
will come to be regarded as a desideratum in itself, and that
things will be produced that do not represent utilities, at
least not utilities toward the attainment of any high ends,
but that rather, in this respect, represent only countless small
futilities.

Nor can the system be self-reforming. If the human and
cultural aridities inherent in it become too obvious, and if
it seeks to remove these, it can bring to the problem of their
removal only the same sort of rationalistic thought that was
unable to lay hold on such values in the first place, and that
therefore erected a system from which such values, while
not deliberately expelled, were yet, by the very nature of the

case, omitted. The only solution, therefore, that industrialism can offer to those who ask that it contribute to human and cultural values, is a further industrialism that will become so efficient and complete that it will efface itself and leave humanity free for more purely human ends. That has ever, indeed, been its hope—a hope that is akin to that of the money-maker, who would amass a fortune that he may be released from material cares. Perhaps the time is even now at hand for such a hope to be fulfilled; but even if it is, we will be slow to recognize it. For even as they progress toward fulfillment, both industrialism and the money-maker alike build up preoccupations, action-patterns, techniques, obligations, and even concrete, substantial holdings, that are not easily disposed of. The moment of fulfillment consequently appears as one of relinquishment, of renunciation, perhaps, even, of flight and of betrayal of solemn trusts. The dismay with which the world now faces a partial retreat from a robust industrial faith, and the sense it gives us of turning from a full and vivid world to one that is somewhat empty and very strange, may possibly be thus explained. In the rational and mechanistic world to which we have become accustomed, we have not been thinking primarily of men as human beings, but have rather considered them as employees and employers, producers and consumers, as an abstraction called the "economic man"—in short as industrial and economic units. The thinking, feeling, willing, human being, full of desires, imaginations, aspirations, of impulses both wayward and noble, of sensibilities both fine and foolish, has not been foremost in our thought. Now we must become acquainted with him again. It will probably take us a long time.

CHAPTER THREE

Education and Modern Thought

Education, since it deals so largely with imponderables not discernible under scientific lenses, might have been expected to escape the limited and special point of view essential to the acquisition of physical knowledge; but it has enjoyed, in fact, no such immunity. That it has not been diverted further than it has from its normal channels is due to our inability to maintain lastingly and in unalloyed form the external view, or (as Dr. Fite comfortably terms it) the "outside" view; and that it has been diverted as much as it has is owing, no less, to the fact that such a viewpoint is certainly not only easy to acquire but has moreover been lately strongly approved and very widely embraced.

Two kinds of testimony

Now, as Dr. Fite [1] says, the "outside" standpoint is that of an observer, and the "inside" standpoint is that of the agent. How it feels to be a child of six years and go to a public school for the first time and receive a first music lesson, and how a child looks to a scientific outside observer under the same circumstances, are bases for vastly different forms of testimony. Accordingly, as we emphasize one point of view or the other in our educational theory and practice, we

[1] *The Living Mind*: Warner Fite.

shall arrive at conclusions that are widely different. Those conclusions are the more annoyingly different, too, because they are disparate rather than opposed or divergent. That is to say, each harmonizes perfectly with its premises, each way of regarding the pupil has authentic basis in our own nature and modes of response, and both sets of conclusions, however disparate they may appear after we have reached them, can consequently lay claim to equal and authentic parentage. Advantage, however, under our modern "intellectual climate," has lain with the "outside" view. The supporters of that are at least able to adduce "facts" in proof of the validity of their claims. However, since their observations in the first place are turned precisely on the factual, as that can be seen and be measured mathematically, the result may not be so surprising or impressive as it might at first glance appear.

On the other hand, there may be ground for surprise over the silence maintained with respect to the disparate doctrine. Surely the "inside" point of view is important in practice if not articulate in theory; for to ordinary observation most of the business of education is in accordance with its implications. Moreover, even were it not valid it would be inescapable, since the teacher who would attempt to approach pupils wholly from the objective standpoint, that is to say, would study them as pedagogical laboratory subjects, and who would assume that the student should similarly regard his instructor and all else in his universe as objects of cold, factual perception, would certainly abruptly lose both pupils and his contract. Yet the adherents of the subjective view, if there be any, have elaborated little defence of their position, and have been able to adduce little in the way of a basic philosophy or pedagogy for its support. Authority held them; the other party had the floor.

They might have observed that the solid and ponderable "facts" gathered by the objectivists elucidate no problems that arise in the field of the teacher's action when that field is imperatively and protractedly held, as it must be, within the subjective view; that such facts, indeed, often appear curiously irrelevant, and sometimes positively distasteful, when viewed from this "inside" standpoint of the needs and trends of pupil development. Without disparaging the truth and value of the testimony brought to them by the objectivists, the subjectivists might have asked whether other orders of truth than the factual may not have foundation and value, whether "facts" are indeed all we can ever know of truth and meaning. But it is hard to withstand the tide of prevailing opinion when that tide has grown to colossal proportions. Of itself it will one day cease to advance, and forces from other directions will then gather to thrust it back. Perhaps such a juncture, speeded by a crisis in our whole basis of civilization, is even now at hand. In that case the idealists may again become articulate.

Objectivism applied to social education

The influence of the "scientific prepossession," as Dr. Fite terms it, may be traced in numerous phases of modern education. In each and all it will tend to direct attention toward the physical and mechanistic features of that which is before it, and will ignore, or else try to lay unaccustomed and ill-fitted hands upon, that which eludes its physical grasp. As Bergson [1] truly says of this way of knowing: "It seems essential to it to measure, and wherever calculation is not yet applicable, wherever it must limit itself to description or analysis, it manages to set before itself only the side which later may become amenable to measurement." This tendency, as we observed it in the preceding chapter, thus gave to society the aspect of a calculable industrial or economic mechanism. Now we would add that it is but a step from that conception to one of education as a mechanistic effort which aims to fit the individual with precision, as a social power-unit, into this "social organism." That such an education may easily move toward mere sophistication, toward pliant acceptance of conventional forms, and toward loss of creative vision to both pupil and teacher, is obvious. Here, however, discussion of its intrinsic worth is no more important than recognition of the philosophical assumptions that gave it birth.

It must be evident that under such a view the social system, like our solar system, is something fixed and given, to the exigencies of which the individual orbit must be bent to conform. With similar mechanistic bias the individual (who now, by the way, begins to lose all that might give him individuality) becomes a unit quite indistinguish-

[1] *Mind-Energy:* Henri Bergson

able from a thousand other units, to be made into the desired configuration by means identical with those that shape all. That "where there is the greatest eccentricity of character there is the greatest genius"—if we are to believe John Stuart Mill; that a social system is first of all an aggregation of individuals whose forms of social relation are dependent upon the degrees and kinds of qualities possessed by the individuals themselves; that the elevation and emancipation of society must therefore depend upon the elevation and emancipation of the individual; and that education should consequently address itself to the quickening of the innermost powers of the individual; these are considerations that are likely to disappear into an obscure background when a too obtuse objectivism holds rule.

Henderson,[1] in writing of this same education toward a social environment, points out the direction that reform must take in these words: "The attempt to erect this environment into something apart from man, as something causative, and to treat it as a "social organism," with specific qualities and powers, seems to me a bit of very empty phrase-making, and productive of far more confusion than enlightenment. . . . Education produces social results of the utmost attainable value, but they are summaries of individual results, not separate group results. In both aim and method, education deals and must deal with individual units. When education deals wisely and efficiently, the total result is good. But whatever the quality of the total result

[1] What Is It To Be Educated: C. Hanford Henderson.

it is precisely the same in kind and degree as the average result achieved in the individual consciousness. To go outside of this consciousness into that vague summary which we call society, is to chase a mirage and lose sight of reality. The current schemes of social education, and the current belief in the fetish of a social organism both rest, it seems to me, upon our growing habit of turning away from the palpitating, immediate integrity of consciousness to the lifeless desert of symbol and metaphor."

If we understand by the "lifeless desert of symbol and metaphor," the region inhabited by such abstractions as the "economic man," the "consumer," or the "industrial unit," we here find ourselves in the realm of the schematic, the realm of the graph, the engineering drawing; and if we understand by the "palpitating immediate integrity of consciousness" the living, human being in all of his human aspects, rather than as seen in some abstract significance, we perceive that we are here simply being counseled to turn from the impersonal, objective view, to the "inside" or subjective view.

The Schematic view

At any point of application the external view thus inevitably tends to present human life in terms of the schematic and regimented. Applied to education it will concern itself more with what human beings are seen to do than with what they may intrinsically be. As a consequence, industrial, vocational and civic education, and education for social utilities, will receive the larger share of its attention. Emphatically it does not, or need not, deny place to moral and aesthetic factors in either life or education. The outward effects and aspects of these, indeed, it may even bring within its field of social study and calculation. But, as we have said before, in its own character it does not lay hold on such essences. It can see men in religion and art, but not religion and art in men; it can discern art and religion in the world, but not a world absorbed in art and religion. Only the objectified, schematically arranged, is shaped to fit its hold.

Education for life

No ideal could be higher than that expressed by the phrase "education for life," provided a sufficiently noble meaning is attached to the word 'life.' What kind of life? Life as it is or life as it should be? Life as externally viewed or life conceived as subjective experience? Such questions as these must be answered before the phrase becomes more than empty rhetoric. And since objectivism has pervaded the thought of the world very extensively for several decades, we must expect to find the definition of life that is now entertained, or at least the unspoken conception of it that is implied in the nature and direction of present educational movements, to be largely influenced by that particular point of view.

"Knowledge is power": so said Francis Bacon, and the saying has been oft and approvingly quoted. But power for what? Power of what kind? Obviously knowledge is not spiritual power, for common observation testifies that spiritual power and knowledge are not related and do not bear any fixed ratio to one another. Nor did the apostle of the inductive method and "the dry light of reason" entertain any such ideas. Knowledge is practical power, power that the rational intellect can use in its mastery of man's environment; and possession of such power by an individual gives him, in turn, another power, namely the power to command an income. Knowledge is marketable. In a scientific age, brought about by ascendancy of the external view, the society generated by that view becomes itself a phenomenon to be studied in the same light, in order that education may receive guidance. It is small wonder that under such conditions education should reveal traces of belief that education for life is education for practical living in a society that is now successfully constituted, and that it should place undue emphasis, at times, upon efficiency, rational power, knowledge, and speed in learning, in distinction to moral qualities, creative thinking, imagination, control and ennoblement of feeling, and direction of taste.

Tests and measurements

The tendency just described may be discerned in that feature of modern educational practice known as tests and measurements. As was said of our material technological improvements and of the entire objective point of view, this feature is not objectionable in itself. It commits sins—at least sins of omission—only when it is elevated to the rank of a philosophic first principle. Only educationists can so elevate it, it is true, and they have not all done so; but it is to be feared that, dominated by our modern "scientific prepossession," many have, at times, nearly approximated such summation.

Intelligence tests

From the point of view we are maintaining, intelligence tests do not measure human values so much as they measure chances in life. The fact that intelligence only is rated—if it is—and that many beautiful qualities and attributes are not investigated, should put us on our guard. For this intelligence is the power by which we act on matter, and it does not lie at the sources of our moral and aesthetic orientations.

From intelligence tests we gather homogeneous groupings. Much might be said concerning the intrinsic worth of these, but for our purpose such discussion would be beside the point. It is enough to point out here that the worth to be discerned among the members of any homogeneous group is not primarily a disposition-worth, or a moral worth, or an aesthetic worth—although a wise and tender Creator might be disposed to consider these—but is a worth measured in terms of ability to acquire knowledge, pass through school, and (probably) get on in the world. Nor is much thought given to the effect upon the sensibilities and ambitions of those placed among the low I.Q's. Perhaps even education for competence is not fully considered. For education is not correctly symbolized by a ladder or vertical line. It has depth, breadth, and richness, as well as linear extent. A fact once learned, a lesson once conned, is therefore not exhausted. Even to that which is familiar something of meaning is added by repetition and review. The play of other minds, too, even if these are less facile, teaches something of human values and qualitative and quantitative abilities, even if it does not add to intellectual grasp of the specific subject matter. And to the less quick of intelligence the association with the more quick must be of untold value.

In the world outside the schoolroom we would think it a calamity never to be associated with any but those of precisely our own degree of understanding and capability. We learn something of life, if not something of the specific problem, by heterogeneity. Within limits, it is true, there must be separation. Abnormal pupils, pupils specially conditioned by physical or psychological abnormalities, must be given an education especially fitted to their condition, just as we segregate the abnormals outside of school. But the fine shading of intelligence often sought in schools betrays a worship of the mechanistic ideal that is distinctly dangerous unless balanced by extraordinary understanding of other human and social values.

Attainment and diagnostic tests

We need not discuss at length diagnostic and attainment tests. Their mechanistic point of view is evident almost in the terms themselves. On the other hand, there is much more to be said in their favor. Application of scientific measurement to attainments is wholly defensible. In life and in school one is expected to attain some goal and produce some product, and it is dishonest and demoralizing to have such products evaluated by diverse and uncertain subjective judgments. The only misfortune here is that the kinds of attainment that are measurable in precise terms are rather blunt and obvious. Whether a person has gained in knowledge of staff-notation may be accurately ascertained, but whether he responds more warmly and deeply to music than he did at an earlier time, or than do others in his class, is hardly to be computed in exact figures. It would be captious, nevertheless, to reject the service that attainment tests can render on the ground that there are other services that they can not render.

Diagnostic tests are less defensible—as they are less reliable—because here, as in intelligence tests, not an objective product but a subjective agent is under examination, and the incorporeal nature of the thing under investigation unfits it for study by genuinely scientific methods. For, we say again, science must demonstrate eventually to the physical senses in order to prove itself scientific, as well as to ascertain whether it has been scientifically right or scientifically wrong—since even to proceed scientifically does not always mean to arrive at a truth. But how can diagnostic testing prove itself, when so much remains invisible? Overt responses at the time there must be, and overt responses in long future there will be; but interest on the part of the subject, that will lead to fidelity in effort and success in accomplishment, can not be measured; and the diagnostic test thus remains a test in native capacities (greatly thinned) and in present power. To forecast the future on such a basis is to make prophecies rather than to lay down scientific certitudes. In any event the diagnosis is concerned with vocational probabilities rather than with human values; and while this is not to its discredit, the reflection is pertinent whenever such diagnosis begins to entrench on human values, or to depart from the realm of the objective and certifiable, to which it is native and in the coin of which the value of its services must be counted.

The scientific spirit and educational psychology

The most grievous results to education of extending the scientific method beyond its proper domain—or else of ignoring as non-existent or chimerical all that is extraneous to that particular domain—become apparent when psychology, in order to prove itself substantial and reputable, becomes scrupulously "scientific." In proportion as it seeks that position it must obviously forsake the psychic and concern itself with the physical because only there can it find the ponderable and measurable factors concerning which it can make affirmations that hold scientific certitude. Accordingly modern psychology has displayed an increasing tendency to relinquish rich territories of specifically psychological inquiry in favor of physiological study and mechanistic experiments. At the same time, since it could not forget that it was, after all, psychology, it has disclosed a still more dangerous tendency to interpret physiological happenings in psychological terms that have often quite over-stepped the limits of the scientifically observable. Thus it has interpreted nerve impulses in terms of sensation and perception, and brain anatomy in terms of mind-analysis, although neither sensation, perception or mind lay on the face of the physiological phenomena. Of this naïve hypothesis we shall speak again in our next chapter.

But meanwhile we must observe that such transgressions from the sphere of science appear in no way to have invalidated as "scientific" the furthest interpretations reached by such methods. Since the beginnings took place in the scientific field, the psychological conclusions were supposed to be similarly solidly scientific. That a gap existed between the two fields, and that it had been blithely leaped instead of solidly filled in to the level of the adjoining sides, was unobserved. The psychologists leaped it because of native and irrepressible psychological leanings. The physiologists failed to observe it, or were not disposed to trouble themselves about it, because the further territory was not theirs, and because, moreover, they were complimented and pleased to find their domain elevated to the rank of a mother country, in relation to which the other territory was a mere dependency, and from which it would draw the raw materials and processes to be used in reconstituting the mind, feelings, and temperaments of its psychological output. So arose a psychological physiology and a physiological psychology that have yet hardly received their due measure of critical scrutiny.

The practical outcome, meanwhile, has been the growth of a tendency to discern in mind no more than could be observed in the body as an organism displaying the operation of physical and chemical forces, and in mental operations no more than could be evaluated in mathematically measurable terms. Such a tendency, we reiterate, is not culpable for what it has produced—for it has actually made contributions of value to our knowledge and competence—but for what it ignores or positively rejects. It forgets or minimizes or repudiates, as in the illustrative figure of "my friend," drawn in an earlier chapter, the "palpitating consciousness," the feeling, willing, personality, that we recognize as the boy or the girl we meet in our homes and on playgrounds. The residue, with which it is admirably fitted to deal, is the physical object that comes to school to be educated. Fortunately we, as teachers, do not limit our ministrations to those phases of being revealed to us by such a purely scientific psychology.

Chapter Four

The Case Against Materialism

Many of the arguments against materialism have necessarily been implied in the foregoing chapters as the negative side to materialism itself; for, as Schopenhauer remarks, "no object apart from a subject can be conceived without contradiction." Much remains, however, that either has not been implied or that needs now more explicit and systematic treatment. In particular, the philosophic doctrine that is in opposition to materialism has not been set forth, and may well receive attention.

External reality and consciousness

The source of materialism is in the idea that the universe presented to the physical senses is Reality. Conceding that that which is so brought to our physical consciousness consists of realities, we must still question, because we find such a universe incomplete and alien, whether it is the full and ultimate Reality; and then, if we are unwilling to accept it as such, we are bound to seek Reality elsewhere.

The quest will begin to show some dawn of promise if we ask what it is that thus affirms reality of something which it, the affirmant, is not. Matter is not itself able to declare itself reality; and what the nature of its reality would be in a universe that held nothing but itself, and in which no part, therefore, was known to any other part, can never be stated. For such a universe would, of course, contain no consciousness; and as conscious beings we are unable to affirm the nature of the unconscious, as the unconscious would exist were there no consciousness to become conscious of it.

The naïve illogic by which pseudo-science has thus ruled consciousness out of that world of which it has become quite acutely conscious is one of the most amazing aspects of modern thought. Were that thought speculative or epistemological the strange conclusion might be regarded as just another philosophical vagary. But modern thought wishes facts and demands proof; and how it can affirm the absence or the existence of consciousness, or anything about consciousness whatsoever, on its premise of a material universe in which consciousness, if hypothesized at all, is certainly not physically discernible, is quite beyond understanding.

Consciousness as Reality

If the physical fact and the conscious fact are disparate, and if the physical fact is not reality, or at least does not present all of reality, are we then to say that the conscious fact is primary and basic, and that consciousness alone is reality? That problem has vexed philosophers from the beginning of philosophic thought. It can hardly be more than posited here, and certainly can not be adequately discussed. Nevertheless, some answer must be attempted.

Ordinary commonsense would appear to support the conclusion that the conscious fact is the primary and basic one because without consciousness there would be no facts. For a fact is a fact only in consciousness or awareness; and while we can still imagine existence without awareness (but only because we *have been* aware, and only in forms such as we have been aware of) we can not affirm it.

On the other hand, consciousness itself is indubitable. We experience it, or, as Bergson says, *live* it, and therefore know it at first hand. It is certainly as real as that which it brings out of the conjectured unknown into the known; that is to say, it is as real as that which it is conscious of. But is it *more* real? Is that which is known not only incomplete and conjectural without the knower, but is it a mere phantasm created by the knower? Here again commonsense intervenes and assures us that we could not be conscious if there were nothing to be conscious of. *Something* is "out there" as a term in the transaction with that which is "in here." Neither appears to have reality—which is to say that either is a pure abstraction—in the complete absence of the other. To be sure, that which is "out there" can be known only in our own terms, that is to say, in terms fixed by our apparatus for knowing, or, in short, the apparatus of our physical senses. From Berkeley and Kant, through Schopenhauer, who begins his work *The World as Will and Idea* with the statement, "The world is my idea," and in and through the writings of countless other philosophers to the present day, runs this clear understanding.

The spectacle of the world that exists in us—and, it is worth while to say here, that does not exist in trees, stones, or parsnips—is not the same one that would exist were our sensory organs changed. Were our eyes those of the fly, were our noses those of the bloodhound, were we possessed of organs of sense such as the antennae of the butterfly, or were we fish or dragon-flies, our universe would be transformed.

The two terms of Reality

We are driven, then, to the conclusion that the external and the internal both exist, and, indeed, quite inescapably imply one another. But this is not to say that the absolute nature of either is thereby affirmed. As Kant remarks: "Nothing which is seen in space is a thing by itself. . . . Objects by themselves are not known to us at all, and what we call external objects are nothing but representations of our senses, the form of which is space, and the true correlative of which, that is the thing by itself, is not known, nor can be known by these representations, nor do we care to know anything about it in our daily experience."

Schopenhauer has much to the same effect, and quotes Sir William Jones [1] as follows: "The fundamental tenet of the Vedanta school consisted not in denying the existence of matter, that is, of solidity, impenetrability, and extended figure (to deny which would be lunacy), but in correcting the popular notion of it, and in contending that it has no

[1] From that writer's *Asiatic Researches*.

essence independent of mental perception; that existence and perceptibility are convertible terms." Obviously this is far from what Bergson mentions as "the tendency of realism to pass beyond what is presented to the mind": and the position is supported by Haldane, who exclaims: "We cannot jump out of our skin of perception to a world which is beyond it."

On the other hand, to deny the absolute nature of knowledge gained through the senses is not equivalent to rejecting or impugning the authenticity of such knowledge. For all practical purposes, and in relation to our highest as well as to our lowest interest, the external may be taken to exist, as Kant implies, precisely as we see it. But we may repeat now, with fuller understanding, the statement relative to "the physical conception of our universe" previously quoted from Haldane: "It embodies a view, though only a very partial view, of actual reality."

Consciousness and physical science

One is not left secure in the position now reached until an assumption often advanced by modern science and complacently accepted as though it were scientifically proven, is overthrown. This assumption is that nerve impulses, and physical and chemical phenomena in our physical organism are the full equivalent of consciousness. Against this extraordinary assumption we may cite William James. James somewhere has a telling statement to the effect that when you have traced the flow of some magnetic current along some gray fibre and have witnessed some molecular changes in some gray matter within the skull, you have nowhere lighted on the poet's dream. Bergson,[1] too, follows the same thought when he says: "Is the mental fact our faculty of perceiving and feeling? Our body, inserted in the material world, receives stimulations, to which it must respond by appropriate movements; the brain, and indeed the cerebro-spinal system in general, is concerned with these movements, it holds the body ready for them; *but perception itself is a wholly different thing.*" (My italics.) Max Müller, in his *Translator's Preface* to Kant's *Critique of Pure Reason,* reiterates the same thought in these words: "But the idea that these physical and physiological researches have brought us one inch nearer to the real centre of subjective perception, that any movement of matter could in any way explain the simplest sensuous perception, or that behind the membranes and nerves we should ever catch hold of what we call the soul, or the I, or the self, need only to be stated to betray its utter folly." The folly, however, has not been so readily perceived. Even psychologists, impelled by the urge to become truly scientific, in a world that recognized no truth but that to which the senses testified, and held to a mechanistic interpretation by such apostasy, have lightly jumped the chasm between the two classes of facts and proclaimed that in physiology could be found the genesis of all conscious life and human behavior. No won-

---

[1] *Mind-Energy:* Henri Bergson

der that Canon Streeter,[1] pondering this materialistic explanation, should have been led to exclaim: "It is odd, too, that a universe that is itself an automaton should give birth to little automata alive enough to know that their life is an illusion."

Unscientific science

Many writers have remarked that science would be quite helpless were it asked to prove scientifically what is accepted nowadays as scientific psychology. Haldane,[2] learned in physiology, biology, psychology, and philosophy, points out that even in physiology we have such facts as repair of injuries, recovery from disease, persistence toward maintaining a given structure, the power to reproduce that structure, constant sustaining of delicate and innumerable relationships between the different parts of the organism and between the organism and all the features of its environment, that collectively represent a movement toward "coordinated maintenance" of life that is wholly different from a series of separate mechanical incidents such as might be observed in inorganic matter. In biology, as might be expected, he finds the mechanistic theory still less applicable to the facts of life, and concludes: "The failure of the mechanistic theory extends over the whole field of the phenomena of life. We can only adhere to this theory if we obstinately close our eyes to facts." In application to psy-

---

[1] *Reality:* Burnett Hillman Streeter.
[2] *Materialism:* J. S. Haldane.

chology he says: "Neither perceptions nor conscious acts of will can by any possibility be described as mere isolated impressions or responses to them. Their place in personality is inherent in them. The physically interpreted universe is only a very partial representation of the universe of our experience, and for the study of psychology is quite insufficient. What Western civilization has come to accept as a common-sense physical universe represents a wholesale abstraction from experience."

Even more convincing, because elaborated from the data of physiological psychology itself, is the testimony of Charles Fox.[1] This writer reviews in detail the physiological machinery of sensations, their stimulus by an electric current, and the measurement of the nerve current by valve amplifiers. He notes that "action is intermittent, and a constant stimulus must produce a series of discrete impulses." He cites the demonstration by Dr. E. D. Adrian of the "all or none" rule, meaning that the strength of a stimulus is sufficient or not sufficient to cause an "impulse *in a single nerve fibre*," but that, once released, the impulse is of one intensity (in one fibre—but other fibres may become engaged) whatever the strength of the stimulus. He observes that this means that the nerve fibre provides its own current and "utilizes all the available resources of the nerve fibre." Further, since muscles may become fatigued "energy is not transmitted from the nerve to the muscle." He finds, however, that the most powerful valve amplifiers fail to show

[1] In *The Mind and Its Body.*

any difference between centripetal and centrifugal currents, between impulses which produce different sensations, as, for instance, visual and auditory. He objects, therefore, not only to saying that the nerves convey sensations, but to saying that they transmit messages; for a message has a definitive form that gives it specific meaning, while these messages are all "of the same simple pattern." He objects even to calling them signals, "for signals must differ if they are to have any significance." He discusses the chronaxies of nerves and the selectivity of paths physically provided by the variety of time constants, and he discusses images, "in the wings, waiting to appear on the stage of consciousness."

His conclusions at this point may be suggested by brief quotations. "It is clear that sensations are not conveyed by nerves, and that living tissue is an essential part of the physical basis of sensation. But the living nervous system simply provides the physiological conditions for the arousal of sensations; whilst the existence of a mind is the essential condition, without which the nerves are powerless." And, further: "Sensations and images are data. We must, as psychologists, start with some material, and these are part of what we start with. They are given in experience and we cannot psychologically go behind them; they are for us ultimate. *Ex nihilo nihil fit.* Unless we have sensations and images we cannot, as psychologists, make any progress. Of course we can investigate the conditions under which they arise, and it is the psychologist's business (unless it is the physiologist's) to do so." He urges, however, that in such investigation the conditions be not considered *causes* any more than the paint, canvas, posing of the sitter, etc., be considered the causes, rather than the conditions, of a portrait. "After we have studied all that physiology can teach us about nervous impulses we are still not a whit nearer the sensation, which is left on our hands unexplained and unaccounted for." He also quotes Professor L. L. Thurstone: "I suggest that we dethrone the stimulus. He is only nominally the ruler in psychology. The real ruler of the domain which psychology studies is the individual and his motives, desires, wants, ambitions, cravings, aspirations. The stimulus is merely the more or less accidental fact in the environment, and it becomes a stimulus only when it serves as a tool for somebody's purposes. It is not a cause. It is simply a means by which we achieve our own ends, not those of the stimulus."

And he arrives at conclusions represented by the following scattered quotations. "Mind and matter are in different categories." . . . "We know the facts of mind by living through them, by subjective experience. We have, in other words, direct insight in this realm, as opposed to inferential knowledge in the other." "The mind that is contemplated when we are dealing with physiological psychology is not the same thing as the mind conceived as subject or ego. Mind is used in two different senses; as what has been called psychoplasm which is associated with and supplies the directing forces of the bioplasm, and which together with it constitutes a unity; *and an ego or subject for whom the unified psycho-bioplasm is an instrument for carrying out his purposes.* When a sensation, for example, arises as the result of stimulating a nerve, this constitutes a modification or change in the psychoplasm. But some subject or ego is aware of this change. The sensation is owned; it does not float about in the world at large, but belongs to some ego. This fact is so necessary that if we attempt to ignore it we are driven to the absurdity of supposing that each separate sensation has its own soul or ego which knows it. *For known a sensation must be."* (The italics are mine.) "Much misapplied ingenuity has been displayed by many psychologists and some philosophers in building up the structure of our knowledge on the basis of material, none of which is known to anybody."

Mind and Brain

One final phase of so-called scientific psychology should be pointedly discussed before we draw larger inferences and proceed to chart our course through other realms. It is the assumption, mentioned earlier, that there exists a parallelism or equivalence between mind and brain. On this point Bergson [1] speaks with penetrating clearness. After mentioning the fact that mechanistic science must measure, and where measurement is not applicable that it examines only that in the subject of study that is amenable to measurement, Bergson continues: "Now it is of the essence of mental things that they do not lend themselves to measurement.

[1] *Mind-Energy:* Henri Bergson.

The first movement of modern science was bound, then, to be to find out whether it was not possible to substitute, for the phenomena of the mind, phenomena which are measurable and which could be their equivalent. Now we see that consciousness has some relation to the brain. So modern science seized upon the brain, took hold of the cerebral fact—the nature of which, indeed, we do not know, but we do know that it must finally resolve itself into movements of molecules and atoms, that is to say, into facts of a mechanical order—and determined to consider the cerebral as the equivalent of the mental." And then he proceeds further to point out that the matter of which the brain is composed does not disclose, at least to science in its present state, changes that correspond completely and at every point to the mind indubitably possessed by the owner. Clearly, science is not prepared to examine a brain and tell us, therefrom, all about the mentality and character of the possessor. It is foiled in the presence of a force which leaves such small, dubious and incommensurable traces in matter.

The reasonable inference is that the mind is not explicable in terms of matter, and that the universe is not wholly or even primarily physical, since it is by this mind, not reached by material science, that we infer its existence at all. The contrary inference, to the effect that the mind, since it eludes the grasp of the physico-chemical realist, must be unreal, a "phosphorescent glow overhanging the dance of the atoms in the brain," and that it may properly be disregarded in substantial scholarly study, is wholly illogical and quite outside the pale of scientific affirmation. Bergson concludes, in substantial agreement with Charles Fox and L. L. Thurstone, as these authors have been quoted, that the brain is merely the instrument by which the ego comes into contact with matter in order to work *its* purposes (*not* resident in the matter) as knowing subject. He would accordingly expect to find in the brain, were our science infinite and therefore capable of finding every smallest trace of change in brain tissue, *not* purposes, preferences, will, thought, but only traces of that which has to do with our action upon our material environment. The brain is thus an instrument, a tool, which reveals the existence of a mind, but that mind is separate from and more than is found in the brain, and "overflows" the brain at every point.

A world with mind and personality added

It remains in this chapter only to sketch the world in which we live as it appears when the objective or realistic outlook is supplanted by one that makes way for mind and personality as unassailable realities known in direct experience. The restoration of such a world would be timely; for lately, due largely to the overthrow of our former systems of physics, and perhaps even more to the bewilderment occasioned by the wholesale break-down of the industrial-economic system which rational thought has erected, dissatisfaction with the entire materialistic regime and distrust of the smug precisianism that buoyed it have been impelling people toward a deeper explanation of life. To pursue our quest we have only to follow further the arguments of Haldane, Fox, and others, as recently adduced. Let us begin again with a single, detached sense-impression. Such a datum, even after it has become known, is something quite without meaning and wholly outside of anybody's experience, although such an abstraction is all that a sense-impression can be to the eye of physical science, because any preference, meaning, motives connected with or aroused by the percept are not on the face of the physical fact. But let Haldane speak further on this.

"In the first place, if all that we perceive consisted of isolated sense-impressions we should have no right, as Berkeley and Hume pointed out, to infer the existence of an external physical world, or, as Hume added, to infer our own existences as anything more than collections of impressions. Kant, who was celebrated alike as a philosopher and astronomer, added a second and far more fundamental criticism. A mere isolated datum of experience is nothing definable or imaginable. Whatever appears to us in our experience appears *as related to other elements in experience.*" (My italics.)

"Each element in our experience embodies significance as entering into our maintained and co-ordinated whole of values, and we can call this whole either our interest or our personality."

"The co-ordination extends, not only over what is ordered spatially around our bodies, but also over what we look back to as in the past and anticipate in the future. Hence the significance of each element in our experience refers to the past and future, as well as to the present, and the values represented in personality extend over the past and future, not merely over the present. We can disregard the values, and we do so in other branches of knowledge; but for a science dealing with conscious experience as such, the fact of their presence cannot be disregarded. They cannot be regarded as merely subjective. Their presence is of the every essence of what is revealed in our universe of experience." [1]

The long chain of what appears to be irrefutable argument by which Charles Fox arrives at a sentient universe cannot be pursued here. Some quotations in the nature of conclusions must suffice. Following directly the quotation from him on pages 41-42 of this book and in line with the foregoing quotations from J. S. Haldane, Fox continues: "If, however, we recognize the ego or subject as an essential constituent in all knowledge or human activity, the problem that confronts us is the relation of this subject to the organized whole composed of mind and body. And the only concepts in terms of which this relationship is describable are spiritual ones, in which all the terms are terms expressing values"; and he adduces approvingly a long quotation from Mr. W. E. Johnson which contains these two sentences: "When objects are characterized by such adjectives as good or beautiful, they can properly be said to be raised

---

[1] In *Materialism:* J. S. Haldane.

into a realm of reality removed from that realm in which reference is made merely to predicates based upon qualities of sensation, or upon the scientifically developed properties of continuants. At any rate these adjectives 'good' and 'beautiful' are imposed upon their objects *in an act which is quite other than the analytico-descriptive* characteristics made by what we call science."

Progressive Humanity

When an ego, with individuality, with selective preferences that work unpredictably in a given environment (as against automatic responses that work predictably), and with the mysterious capacity to attach meanings and values to what otherwise appear on the surface as mere physiological registrations, is thus posited as existing above and beyond the physically discernible—and we must so posit it if we resolutely face all the facts—the face of our world becomes subtly transformed. Human values, as contrasted with values produced by human labor again emerge. Henderson [1] pithily said: "If Man is the highest product of creation, then civilization must be judged, not by what man produces, but by the manner of man produced." A civilization that has unconsciously fallen into materialism has disregarded this axiomatic truth, in practice if not in theory, and has judged itself by its mass production. Haldane,[2] speaking of the same materialistic view, says: "In the grey

[1] *Education and the Larger Life:* C. Hanford Henderson.
[2] J. S. Haldane: *Op. cit.*

light of this realism spiritual values seemed to melt away from the visible world, as the fantastic appearances of night melt away at dawn; but only to leave a drab world of physical and economic reality." But under the later view such lost spiritual values are restored; and they are perhaps all the stronger because they have now had to overcome much that seemed to disprove their claims. Never, indeed, have they been abandoned in fact, because man could not, by the most obstinate adherence to a schematic plan of knowledge he had formed, divest himself, any more than could a Scrooge, of interests and capacities that overflowed the boundaries of his scheme. So we have had art, have had moral aspiration, have had religion, but only as arising from the play of intuition and not as resting upon the most enduring foundations attainable by our highest reason.

The reasoned adoption of a new and broader philosophy, therefore, were it possible, would be an event of first importance; for to go one's way as a matter of sheer gratification of one's interests, without reasoned justification, is vastly less satisfying and noble than to go one's way believing that in so doing one not only satisfies one's desires but pursues a way of highest truth and light. And this holds for a nation as for an individual. A feeling that life is baseless, that it lacks direction and meaning, that it is not whole and integrated, comes to either the individual or the nation whose practices are not buttressed by some adequate principles consciously accepted. Our national life has possibly held some disquieting and feverish qualities because the dominant tenets in our philosophy were not broad enough and rich enough to justify much that our souls still longed for and our hands still sought to grasp. Even those who lived and worked in the fields of morals, religion, and the arts, often felt that they were possibly no more than decorative factors on a real world of solid industrialism, rather than integral factors in a world that embraced purposes that to them seemed of higher importance. These, now, may find justification for their work, beyond the fact that they personally like it. And if to their reassurance should be added a genuine faith on the part of the public in imponderable human values, whether or not these ever turn any scales in the market place, a robust art, with its roots sunk deep in the common soil of its native country, might gradually come into being.

The words with which Charles Fox ends his admirable treatise may fittingly be quoted in closing this section:

"If the view I have put forward is well founded, when a man contemplates the world of values the permanent effects on him are purely subjective. His being is steeped and dyed in what he experiences; so that nobility of soul arises from the pursuit of what is of permanent worth. And it is the destiny of man to foster such commerce with ultimate values in the confident hope that what is so acquired, as it does not depend on the body, can never pass away."

AN AESTHETIC BASIS

Chapter Five

The Nature and Value of Aesthetic Response

Two modes of attention

If, instead of projecting ourselves into the objective world that we might master it, we should accept ourselves as the central fact and allow the world to enter us, for our delight and understanding, then we should have exchanged the factual for the meaningful, the "practical" for the aesthetic attitude. As Prall [1] reasons at the beginning of his book, *The Aesthetic Judgment,* this attitude is precisely all that would be left for us, were the aims of our science, technology, and economics at last fully attained, with the result that every practical end now forecast as desirable would be at our command. Then, like the Almighty, when He made the earth, being beyond the reach of want or self-interest, we could seek, as He did, only for some lovely perfection that would give joy to our spirits. So must He have flung the arch of the heaven, dropped the tinted rainbow down the sky, fashioned the pale moon, mirrored flowers in water, and tossed the butterfly into the sunlight. So could we look upon all these and see, as He did, that they were Good.

[1] *The Aesthetic Judgment:* D. W. Prall.

But lacking fulfillment, and having multifarious needs and desires, we chafe and strive toward attainment after attainment, hoping thus to outstrip our wants.

Now to some extent each one of us participates in both of these phases of experience. Even if, being aesthetically flaccid, we sink into mere day-dreaming, as when idly watching clouds in a summer sky, we still catch some measure of the detachment from insistent circumstance and the sensibility to things as they are that are distinguishing marks of aesthetic response. The sharp *tension* of mind that Bergson truly identifies with *attention,* and which we use when we examine objects with a view to acting upon them practically, is in this case replaced by a state in which the mind embraces rather than scrutinizes the object.

It is true that absorption and conception at the low level mentioned are neither very deep nor very meaningful. But at the highest levels of aesthetic response, something very like complete grasp and innate understanding ensue. In the first case we perceive, in the second case we intuit: and naked perception will have to do with the factual, while intuition will reach behind the observable for essences and meanings. The parallel with the "objective" *versus* the "subjective," as discussed in preceding pages, is obvious. Bergson [1] emphasizes the difference between the two modes of apprehending by this illustration: "Our eye perceives the features of the living being, merely as assembled, not as mutually organized. The intention of life, the simple move-

---

[1] *Creative Evolution:* Henri Bergson.

ment that runs through the lines, that binds them together and gives them significance, escapes it. This intention is just what the artist tries to regain, in placing himself back within the object by a kind of sympathy, in breaking down, by an effort of intuition, the barrier that space puts up between him and his model." Prall [1] uses a similar illustration: "In fact, if attention is characteristically perceptive and not intuitive, these further processes [2] remain largely in abeyance, as when in musical dictation one hears so well as to write out accurately what was perceived through the ears and the sense for rhythm, without in the least feeling the formal or sensuous or expressive beauty of the dictated passage."

It is significant that both of these writers turn to the artist for their illustration of that kind of knowing which is not dependent upon rational power. It emphasizes the fact that a state of culture based wholly upon a belief in the rationalistic will never, of its own volition, comprehend and make provision for a basic place for the arts. It should be observed, too, that the characteristic movement of "perceptive attention," according to these illustrations, is in the direction of analysis, while the characteristic movement of intuition—or shall we say art?—is in the direction of synthesis. The physiologist thus becomes anatomist, and integrates his facts only in the sense of finding laws that move all the anatomical parts in some mysteriously coordinated

[1] *Aesthetic Judgment:* D. W. Prall.
[2] See pages 56-61.

way. The artist, on the contrary, not only sees his subject at the beginning as a unified form, but sees it further as bodying forth some essence of personal or spiritual meaning that possesses—nay, that *is* in itself—complete unity.

Things as related to us, or to one another

Further aspects of these two ways of looking at the world about us deserve notice. All that breaks upon our sensorium and gains the threshold of our attention may come to us as related to ourselves, as having some bearing upon our advantage, our welfare, our purposes or designs. On the other hand we may regard any object as a *thing in itself*, of more or less attractiveness simply *as* an object which we may continue to regard; and its attractiveness in this latter case will be dependent, not upon its relation to our practical interests, but upon its relations to its environment or setting, in terms of symmetry, color, balance, divine fitness; or else upon the relations of its parts to one another, in precisely those same terms. The ultimate reward, in the case of practical meaning, is clearly the satisfaction of some desire, the attainment of some practical end; in the second case the meaning is quite different, and the reward one may experience is simply the joy of beholding. Here, then, we find the basis for the claim, frequently advanced, that art is "disinterested," or unselfish. If we reflect further that the joy of contemplation, of intuition of loveliness, is one that the individual experiencing it is always moved to share, and that possession of it by one does not conflict with possession of it by others, but rather that a community of appreciation is a further delight, we may see the basis of Tolstoi's statement: "The purpose of business is to get; the purpose of art is to give."

Not only do we live at times in one and at times in the other of these modes, but they are likely to combine, or to alternate quickly, in any one incident of our experience. The craftsman makes a chair. In so far as he is preoccupied with thoughts of its monetary value, or of the time and effort he must give to making it substantial in construction and therefore in value, or to the comfort he will derive from sitting in it, he is merely a workman with more or less of conscience. But if he be a true craftsman, these matters are but a small portion of his concern. Any one of countless forms and sizes of legs would make the chair substantial; scant thought would be needed to make it salable; a few simple features would make it comfortable. But the grain of the wood, which has no connection with the physical comfort the chair may offer, is likely to be a matter of long consideration; the curve of a line that has no structural significance may occupy loving thought for days; the very shade of the finish, and whether that finish shall be dull or bright, are momentous questions to be deliberated long after considerations of strength, comfort, and market value, have been met and passed. "That search for seductive forms which is art," according to Balzac, must still allure the artist that is in the craftsman. And labor though he may in this latter service, he feels his labor rewarded if and when he finds the elusive grace he sought; and shirk though he may, in the service of quick and easy profit, he finds such lesser labor curiously vexatious and unrewarded. The only lure it holds is the hope that it may bring him such financial return that in the end he may escape it and thenceforth do as he would.

Present and future reward

When artists of all kinds work in this way, to relate line to line, mass to mass, color to color, word to word, tone to tone, in some form that, out of tempting mists, beckons them onward till they make ecstatic discovery of it, they reach at once that end—which is a present full measure of pure joy and satisfaction—that is the ultimate object of all our practical striving. For the useful things that we strive after and call good are good for something; and that something is, in the last end, a something that will give pleasure in feeling. They are thus not ends in themselves, but means. Vernon Lee [1] points this distinction between 'good' and 'beautiful'—which is familiar enough in aesthetics—by comparing the good road with the beautiful road. The good road is one that enables us to travel over it and get to the end of it and off of it—or at least to the end of some part of it. It has no charm in itself, but promises to conduct us to a situation that will charm, or that perhaps will enable us to reach a still further situation, or a chain of them, where charm will finally await. The beautiful road, on the

[1] *The Beautiful:* Vernon Lee.

contrary, is a present satisfaction. It promises nothing, leads us to no place so charming as itself. We linger with it in contemplation, leave it with reluctance. It is present payment; the practical "good" is a promise to pay. So, to a world that, by means of myriad utilities and conveniences, has been led to press ever more strenuously toward a goal that has as quickly receded to a further point, the consciousness of a universe already made, that holds delights on every hand would we but cease from looking over and beyond them, may prove a blessing.

The depth and amplitude of aesthetic response

One may look at the moon and affirm that it is round, or may gaze on it and observe that it is beautiful. In either case, to use Prall's [1] convenient term, a transaction has taken place, as between subject and object, between observer and observed, between something here and something there. But what is the difference between the two transactions that leads to the difference in testimony? Assuming, as we must, that it was the same moon in both cases, that is to say, that the objective term of the transaction was constant, what were the variable factors in the subjective term?

When one says, then, that the moon is round, he records a testimony that rests upon perceptive attention, or, viewed from a slightly different angle, upon sensory experience. The testimony is factual, rational. It implies no organic engagement beyond that ordinarily connected with visual per-

[1] *The Aesthetic Judgment:* D. W. Prall.

ception. But while one can say that visual perception alone gives rise to the testimony that the moon is round, he can hardly contend that visual perception in itself includes factors that give rise to the testimony that the moon is beautiful. Even a materialist who would maintain that the bare optical mechanism, without sentience behind it, could register roundness, could surely find no ground for contending that it could register beauty. Indeed, he would probably scout the idea that beauty exists at all, anywhere, for the precise reason that he could not find it on the retina. Nevertheless, to any one but an utter materialist, the two testimonies must alike appear as subjective responses. And the difference between them appears to be, so far as we have now inquired, that the one, as to the fact of roundness, engaged the subject somewhat partially, perhaps even superficially, while the other, as to beauty, engaged him more deeply, reverberated through more of his being and, in some way, through deeper and less easily and frequently resonated parts of his being. For, as Dr. P. P. Claxton, speaking of this difference in responses, once said in an address: "We know little, as psychologists, about the feeling; but this we do know, that it lies far deeper than articulate thought."

We can come upon this same view of aesthetic response by another path. A long quotation from Dr. Richard Cabot [1] puts the point vividly. Dr. Cabot says: "To ignore the romance in love, in history, in games, in music, or any-

[1] *What Men Live By:* Richard C. Cabot, M.D.

where else, is one of the easiest things in the world. One
has only to slouch because one is sick of standing erect, to
refuse the task of looking behind the obvious and relapse
into sleepy literalism. As one's eyes grow fatigued with reading, the letters cease to be symbols and become letters only.
Meaning, interest, and *beauty* die out of the words on the
page. They are only printer's type, no longer sign posts to
infinite meaning. . . . A baby is a lump of flesh, a symphony is a long confused noise, a picture is a bit of dis-
colored canvas, a man is an ugly, featherless biped, to any
one who has not interest enough to see more." (My italics.)

Further, Dr. Cabot writes: "To all of us, when we are
sleepy or seasick, the world presents itself in these terms.
Now and then Mr. Shaw attracts notice by loudly exclaim-
ing, in print, that a man can see best when his eyes are too
sleepy to open, and that under these conditions he sees no
romance in the world. . . . By being just a trifle more *blasé*
than Mr. Shaw one can wipe science, mathematics, color,
and shape out of the world. All the experiences of our devitalized moods are flat, colorless, meaningless, and stale,
and it is as easy to let ourselves get devitalized as it is to
drop our end of the load which we are helping to carry."

The aesthetic or feeling reaction is here painted as spring-
ing from sources or vitality not tapped in our ordinary
perceptive experience. The feeling of interest, significance,
meaning, affection, with which one beholds the object is
also rightly recognized as attaching to the true scientific
outlook no less than to the artistic. But while scientific in-

terest brings with it affective reactions that are indubitably
of pure aesthetic character, in any proper sense of the term,
the coldly external view which has been described in these
pages does not entail such aesthetic response. And the point
is important: for it is a matter of common experience that
our ability to perceive the colorless facts remains unim-
paired after the ability to perceive any meaning or interest
in them has departed. Thus we could still perceive that
the moon was round, or curiously marked, or at a particular
angle above the horizon, after we were too exhausted, from
loss of sleep or other cause, to react to its beauty or find
food for reflection in the scientific facts. Or a man who was
weak unto death might perceive his friend at his bedside,
but perceive him only as a size and a shape, blocking out
space. Tennyson, with a poet's divination, penetrates such
a state when he sings:

> Ah, sad and strange as in dark summer dawns
> The earliest pipe of half-awaken'd birds
> To dying ears, when unto dying eyes
> The casement slowly grows a glimmering square.

So, if the mental and spiritual vitality is at a sufficiently
low ebb—and it is worth while to observe that *physical*
vitality is not the efficient agent, as any healthy imbecile
would prove—the casement window is but a lighted
rectangle.

Perception reduced to such a rudimentary state is almost
perception without a perceiver. It is, in fact, precisely that,

for it is perception by only a fraction of a perceiver, or, in other words, is a transaction between an objective and a subjective in which the latter is greatly reduced and largely inert. If we believe, as Bergson and others hold, that the physical senses and the rational intellect constitute a mechanism for acting on matter—though in obedience to a personality that, behind matter, is prompting action—we can account further for the persistence of this factual perception to the very end of vitality. For the material facts so discerned, down to the door of death, are simply the facts essential to the support of animal existence. First to emerge, and granted to lowest intelligence, they are last to disappear. If there be a hierarchy of subjective responses, above them would appear the perception that moves to rational interpretation, to calculation of physical causes and effects with an eye to future material welfare. But surely, if there be a hierarchy of subjective reactions, above this would come the aesthetic response that divines and interprets. And the justification for giving it such place is that, precisely as the second stage of response is deeper and more ample, and includes within it the first without impairment, so does the last appear as of yet greater depth, magnitude, and intensity, and as readily including within itself, without impairment, the capacities of the second.

For it is a mistake to suppose that the rational mind grows blind as the aesthetic regard grows vivid. Violent passions, emotions of rage and despair, can blind the intellect, and superficial thought has assumed that sensitivity to beauty, as an emotion, is similarly correlated with blindness to facts. But this is clearly a popular fallacy that proves itself oblivious to facts. No one, surely, who has been ordinarily observant would claim that the acoustician hears more when a symphony is played, or hears it more accurately, than the musician; or would claim that the astronomer sees the moon more reliably and accurately than the painter. Vague, impressionistic gazing of an aesthetic character there may be, but also there may be very incomplete and inaccurate factual observation. We are justified in believing, however, that mature and competent aesthetic reaction will be found to include an attention to objective features as meticulous as that which characterizes the "objective" type of observation; and in addition there will be a warmth of understanding that lifts the experience to a plane of high significance and value. Without this factor of significance, we may add, there is moreover no conceivable value in having any perception whatever. A fact that has no meaning—and meaning is indefinable except in terms of human interests, wishes, dreams, satisfactions—can hardly be said to be a fact. It is but an event, and that in a conjectural, unconscious, physical world.

Comparative validity of the two testimonies

The knowledge any ordinary man has of what goes on within him is probably sufficient to gain his assent to the statement that aesthetic response is something deeper and more inclusive than factual observation. It is more difficult, however, even for an artist to believe always that the testimony, "the moon is beautiful," is equally valid with the testimony, "the moon is round." One source of the difficulty lies in the fact that concurrence of opinion, or agreement in testimony—usually a factor in establishing validity—is likely to be far less marked in one case than in the other. All of the inhabitants of the artist's town would probably be ready to declare with him that the moon was round; but in all probability they would assent far less confidently, and with more varying degrees of emphasis, that might even shade over into doubt and positive denial, to his statement that it was beautiful. Such differences in conviction—and they appear in connection with all aesthetic matters—are likely to create an impression that aesthetic reaction is capricious, uncertain, imaginary, and even hypocritical. Moreover, the testimony of the aesthetically responsive individual himself varies at different times. The moon, one affirms, is beautiful now; but a violent toothache or a fall in a muddy pool can quite readily cause the affirmant to lose all sensitiveness to its beauty. It may then appear even baleful. However, through all these experiences it does continue, with most annoying pertinacity, to be round. Such unchanging persistence in what we have termed the factual, as compared with the vagaries that we are bound to observe in connection with the aesthetic, gives rise in most minds to a strong presumption of much greater reliability as attaching to the factual.

The case is not, however, so hopeless as at this point it might appear. We must not forget, in the first place, that even the testimony 'round' is subjective and in terms of our subjective organism. The testimony 'beautiful' is not more subjective except in the sense that a larger part of the subjective organism takes part in the transaction; but it would be difficult to prove that the additional subjective participants—let us say glands, or whatever physiological psychologists wish us to believe are the factors that make for the added affective and intuitional processes—are less real and dependable respondents than the original optical ones. They are merely less frequent respondents (especially in aesthetically insensitive persons) and ordinarily do not rouse themselves to participation except in cases of extreme excitation. The artist, drugged with fatigue from loss of sleep, who could still see that the moon was round, and could map its surface or figure its parallax but could not respond to its beauty, would therefore not be giving more truthful testimony about the moon, but merely less complete testimony about it. We would have again, in his factual report, merely that "very partial view of actual reality" of which Haldane spoke. Only when he could, in addition to such a report, testify to its beauty, in terms eloquent of a very real experience, would we have the larger truth.

From this point of view the persistence and stability of the bare and arid factual appears as a deficiency. As Dr. Cabot says, when we are not fully alive we can see no more than these stark percepts. The illusion that such uninviting starkness is reality is due to the fact that we can not sink to a plane of devitalization where at least *that* much fruit of perception will not remain. Such, we may conjecture, is the origin of the realism that has spread into every department of art at various times. The world, the heavens, man and his life, regarded with a hard, objective gaze, scrutinized with the cold stare that marks the absence or the resolute suppression of deeper subjective participation, are held out naked to our gaze by these artists of the realistic school. Sentimentality and a precious hyper-aestheticism, which have occasionally existed, may be false and distasteful, but they are surely neither more false or more repugnant to a healthy nature than this systematic and misguided denudation of life.

CHAPTER SIX

Some Features of Musical Aesthetics

A discussion of aesthetics by Mr. Santayana [1] provides us with a peculiarly convenient and effective basis for our restricted inquiry. Mr. Santayana discusses art under the three main captions, *Material, Form,* and *Expression.* That is to say, all art takes some *Material* or other—as clay, marble, gold, pigments, fabrics, tones, words; fashions the material into some *Form* or other; and the material, so formed, seems to have peculiar and individual character or significance; seems, in other words, to address us with some unique sort of *Expression.*

The effect of Tone

In common with all writers, Mr. Santayana recognizes that the effect of material alone, which, in the case of musical art, is *Tone,* is directly upon the senses. The low sound of a pure-toned bell is thus, to an infant as to an adult, an aesthetic event, needing no knowledge, no persistent attention, to give it charm and peculiar effect. Tone, separated from any musical form or design, is comparable, in such effect upon the senses, to color as detached from graphic form. It evokes a direct and unpremeditated response, to

[1] *The Sense of Beauty:* George Santayana.

which we bring nothing but sensitivity. It would be a grave mistake, however, to underestimate the importance of this aesthetic appeal because it is elementary. On this point Santayana is singularly penetrating and eloquent. "Sensuous beauty is not the greatest or most important element of effect, but it is the most primitive and fundamental, and the most universal. There is no effect of form which an effect of material could not enhance, and this effect of material, underlying that of form, raises the latter to a higher power and gives the beauty of the object a certain poignancy, thoroughness, and infinity which it otherwise would have lacked. . . . And another point. The wider diffusion of sensuous beauty makes it as it were the poor man's good. Fewer factors are needed to produce it and less training to appreciate it. . . . Such simplicity is not the absence of taste, but the beginning of it. . . . The beauty of material is thus the groundwork of all higher beauty, both in the object, whose form and meaning have to be lodged in something sensible, and in the mind, where sensuous ideas, being the first to emerge, are the first that can arouse delight." [1]

It may be well to elaborate this point, further, because musicians and teachers of music themselves persistently overlook the aesthetic importance of tone. In part this is due to the fact that they have moved far beyond the sensory state and have come to concentrate their attention upon the further and larger values of form and expressive

[1] Santayana: *op. cit.*

characteristics. In part, also, it is due to somewhat hasty and incomplete introspection, which leaves them under the impression that the larger values upon which they concentrated their attention were the sole source of their aesthetic reactions. But some reflection, more careful introspection, and some observation of audiences, will tend to correct such an impression. Surely any musical form, however noble, were it given an ugly tonal investiture—as, let us say, the Bach-Wilhelmj *Air for G-string* played upon a strident and scratchy violin—would lose all nobility, and become acutely displeasing to musicians or to a lay-audience alike. Nor would the most impassioned dramatic song, such as the *Libestod* from *Tristan,* be other than offensive raving, if beauty of tone, from both voice and orchestra, were cast aside. Observation will convince the student, too, that a single rich, mellow, chord played by an orchestra will often evoke a rapt, silent, attention from an audience, even of musicians, that no delineation of form or fervency of emotional portrayal had called forth. One must conclude, in the light of these facts, that lovely tone is not only a delight in itself but that it is prerequisite to any and all other effect. It is, indeed, a sensitizing agent, without which the photographic plate of our feeling is not prepared to receive and record other values. It is a mistake to ignore it or take it for granted, and then concentrate all artistic thought elsewhere—a mistake for the artist or hearer, and a greater mistake for the teacher.

The effects of musical Form or Design

It is not necessary, in addressing musicians and music students, to enter into a comprehensive examination of musical form and its aesthetic effect, but certain special aspects of the problem should receive attention. In the first place it is important that we recognize the complete correspondence, the unitary nature, of form and aesthetic effect. It may seem strange that anyone could possibly overlook so obvious a fact; but students of music are, on the one hand so accustomed to regard musical form and forms from a wholly objective standpoint, as matters of technical study, and on the other so often take their own aesthetic responses for granted, as some vague natural result of being musical, that just as they overlook the effect of tone, so they fail to discern the effects of form; and they thus continue aesthetically sensitive while they remain aesthetically unseeing. Were this the case with performing artists alone, there would be small cause for concern: but when one teaches, his selection of music, his methods of presenting the music, his instructions to the performers, all require that he recognize the true bases of musical effect.

It will clarify the point we wish to make if we cease to speak of form, which is likely to call up thought of extended forms, and speak rather of design. Moreover, under that term we shall include not only rhythmic and melodic characteristics, but all other factors that help to make any bit of musical utterance just what it is, such as tone-color, pitch, dynamic shading, and harmony. So understood, we can see that the smallest unit of design, and the slightest detail of pitch-registration or other factor within that unit, give us, whether we are conscious of it or not, the characteristic color of our response in feeling. For instance, were the notes of the famous initial motive of Beethoven's

Symphony in C-minor, not , but

, or and were

it announced by wood-winds, or in another octave, we would be ushered into halls of tone perhaps as spacious and perhaps as impressive, but subtly and yet vitally different in character. Or, if we do not feel so, we may be sure that the composer would have so felt, and that his architectural lines and the feeling they would consequently have created would have been modified throughout. If this be true, then to reach for the meaning of the symphony as a whole (and perhaps find in it the struggle of a soul with fate) without having first become conscious of the nature of the impact thus made upon feeling by the contour and rhythm of each motive and each phrase, as they follow one after the other, is as though one should try to carry a general impression away from a Shakesperian tragedy without having felt the force of any of its lines in particular.

Form as impressive and expressive

In connection with quite small elements of design, to which for a time we wish to restrict our discussion, form, then, *is* the aesthetic effect. Just as the yielding curve of a distant hill of one of the Sierras, or the implacable thrust of the Matterhorn against the sky, awakens a quality of feeling that can only be described in terms of the lines themselves, so the motive from the *Fifth Symphony,* the swelling trumpet note that begins the *Rienzi Overture,* the descending *pizzicati* from the basses, against rising, questioning chords above, in the opening measures of the second movement of Schubert's *Unfinished Symphony,* are contours and movements that speak to our feeling simply in terms of such contours and movements. Lights, shades, colors, are there also, to impress us, as they exist and play likewise upon the Sierras or upon the Matterhorn. They reinforce, or modify, they agree with or oppose, the speech of the lines; but that warm sunlight on a forbidding peak should seem to contradict the expression of the peak itself, is testimony to the explicit quality of the language spoken by the gaunt lines themselves.

Such direct effect, characteristic of small units of musical design, has all the immediacy and the definiteness of quality that we find in sensuous effects. It is a question, then, if form, in any presentation so simple or so small that it enters our consciousness unified and whole, does not affect the senses just as does material, instead of awaiting those higher and more elaborate processes that underlie our aesthetic response to form in larger and more complex presentations. It is a point we need not labor here.

Of more importance, however, is the question as to whether the affective quality so resident in the design—say in the Beethoven motive quoted—not only influences our feeling, but is the essential and complete *expression* of the music. Here again Santayana's [1] statement is classical. He writes: "It would be pedantic, perhaps, anywhere but in a treatise on aesthetics, to deny to this quality the name of expression; we might commonly say that the circle has one expression and the oval another. But what does the circle express except circularity, or the oval except the nature of the ellipse? Such expression *expresses* nothing; it is really *im*pression. . . . We shall accordingly take care to reserve the term 'expression' for the suggestion of some other and assignable object, from which the expressive thing borrows in interest; and we shall speak of the intrinsic quality of forms as their emotional tinge or specific value." Gurney, in his monumental work,[2] discusses the same thought in relation specifically to music, and goes further, in the following words: "But the great point, which is often strangely ignored, . . . is that *ex*pressiveness of the literal and tangible sort is either *absent or only slightly present* in an immense amount of *im*pressive music; that to suggest describable images, qualities or feelings, known

---

[1] *Op. cit.*
[2] *The Power of Sound:* Edmund Gurney.

in other experiences, however frequent a characteristic of Music, *makes up no inseparable or essential part of its function;* and that this is not a matter of opinion, or of theory as to what should be, but of definite everyday fact." (The later italics are mine.)

Now Gurney, in saying that music is characteristically and properly an *im*pressive art—a statement in which practically all writers on musical aesthetics agree—mentions also that the fact is "often strangely ignored." That mention concerns us intimately here. For just as musicians and teachers of music have overlooked the importance of *tone* as a factor in aesthetic effect, so have they overlooked this *impressive* effect, which we see now as synonymous with the effect of design or form; and they have therefore tried too frequently to interpret music wholly or chiefly as expressive, without being very clear as to just what was expressed or as to how the music managed to express it. Or if musicians have not been guilty of this aesthetic shortsightedness, those legions of the public that entertain a wistful or a determined desire to appreciate music have been so. What musician has not at some time been approached by such a seeker with the inquiry: "What does that music mean?" Only politeness, in such cases, prevents the response: "It means just what you hear it say when it is sounding. Listen! . . ." Explicitly, from this point of view, the *Fifth Symphony,* of Beethoven, expresses something in C-minor; something that appears to need rather insistent reiteration; something that moves restlessly, urgently, but "without joy"; that now thunders, now whispers, now gropes, now moves confidently; that is compounded of sounds by flutes that express flute-meanings; of sounds by timpani that express timpani-meanings; of sounds by trumpets and horns that voice trumpet-meanings and horn-meanings. If we seek more explicit "explanation" than this we shall probably descend for it. As Clive Bell [1] says, when condemning himself for aesthetic flaccidity at a concert: "Incapable of feeling the austere emotions of art, I begin to read into the musical forms human emotions of terror and mystery, love and hate, and spend the minutes, pleasantly enough, in a world of turbid and inferior feeling. . . . I know very well what has happened. I have been using art as a means to the emotions of life and reading into it the ideas of life. I have tumbled from the superb peaks of aesthetic exaltation to the snug foothills of warm humanity."

The profound, exalted, absorbing impressiveness that characterizes the works of Bach, Haydn, Mozart, Beethoven, Brahms, and countless others of earlier and later times, and of lesser degree, might well be considered *expressive,* with respect alike to variety, explicitness, and depth of expression. But in an age of material preoccupations, that which the music of those masters expressed is not sufficiently tangible. Their works expressed ideal beauty, ideal motion. The tones that in such music shout to one another across the pages, or whisper mysteriously of the passionless ab-

[1] *Art:* Clive Bell.

sorptions of another world, are disembodied voices, that hold no commerce with earth. Only lately has music been asked to cease to reflect such a world, and discourse instead on our railroads and afternoon promenades. True, it may do this and yet remain good music; but its spiritual height must thereby inevitably be lowered. When pedagogy aids this errant aesthetic notion by inventing for children programmatic explanations of lovely music, and when psychology supports the idea by chronicling, as though it were important, what wayward visions may wander through the minds of unmusical persons while music is entering their hearing, the prospect that any music shall be interpreted on sheer musical grounds becomes unhappily remote.

Expressive music

What has been said may appear to deny any proper place, or even any real existence, to an expressive function of music, when "expressive" is thus defined as connoting effects gained by reference to experiences that lie outside the experience of the music itself, as something heard. But such a position would be foolish and untenable. All opera, oratorio, and song-literature, and the magnificent literature of romantic and programmatic instrumental music, rises to oppose the thought. The point we wish to make, however, is not that such music does not exist, and not that such function is either wholly fanciful or is anti-musical, but that *music does not exist essentially or primarily for such function, and that we are under an illusion when we think that either the significance of a piece of music or its effect upon us is defined largely in such terms.* This amounts to saying that the expressive effect (under our definition of expressive) is an added and somewhat extraneous effect; and this assertion is easily proven. A Chopin nocturne is not enjoyable because it is a nocturne but because it is beautiful music. Any music student might go into a twilight reverie and while in it produce a nocturne, but his evening mood, however commendable, would not guarantee a composition that anyone would care to listen to. So he might essay a *Scheherezade;* but it is likely that the world might prefer to listen to Rimsky-Korsakoff's music, *even were the title of that piece mislaid and its program forgotten,* rather than listen to the student's effusion, though the latter desperately punctuated every measure of it with vivid, point-to-point-correspondence, programmatic notes.

That beauty and high significance and meaning in an art-work are thus not dependent upon "associated" interests extraneous to the work itself has been commonly recognized among writers on aesthetics, and the point would not need elaboration except for a pedagogical application that later we shall wish to make. Nor should we understand that the problem arises only in connection with music. Artists and writers on pictorial art deplore that taste which seizes on the "representative" or "illustrative" aspect in a painting, while remaining insensible to the sheer beauty that is quite independent of the subject. Clive Bell [1] finally defines art as

[1] *Op. cit.*

"significant form" and distinguishes the "emotions of life" from the "emotion of beauty." Nevertheless, in musical as in other art, there is, as Gurney [1] urges, "a difference between music which is expressive in the sense of definitely suggesting or inspiring images, ideas, qualities, or feelings belonging to the region of the *known* outside music, and music which is *not* so expressive"; although in the same connection this writer also says—and it is a point that perhaps needs emphasis above that which we have given it: "We often call music which stirs us more *expressive* than music which does not; and we call great music *significant,* or talk of its *import, . . .* without being able, or dreaming we are able, to connect these general terms with anything *expressed* or *signified."*

We will come close to the heart of the matter if, besides agreeing that expressiveness is a quality separate from musical beauty and even from musical eloquence, we regard it as a specific cast or mood given to eloquence. A work by Bach is thus beautiful and eloquent without having the specific cast that would lead us to call it expressive. Similarly, the works of Haydn and Mozart, in general, are not characteristically expressive, in this limited sense of the word. With Beethoven, however, we come upon many instances of works that disclose an intention to portray some specific and even some individual and perhaps transient mood. More than once, moreover, as in the *Eroica* and the

[1] *Op. cit.*

Pastoral symphonies, an objective basis for the mood is either suggested or explicitly avowed. Unconscious revelation of personality or of a pervasive state of feeling, which we find in Bach and Mozart, is thus displaced by conscious expressive intention. In later days the specific feelings arising from circumstance come more and more to be the basis of composition; and finally, as in *Pacific 231,* music would almost delineate circumstance and incident itself.

Kinds of values

Now a composition is not a masterpiece because it abstains from any expressive or programmatic suggestion, nor is it a botch because it avows extreme programmatic intention. In either case it must be judged, and must lay any claim it may have to survival, solely on the ground of its sheer musical worth. Unquestionably, however, the composer of music of programmatic character will be in danger of overlooking musical values in the pursuit of exciting realistic effects; and quite as certainly the composer of absolute music is in danger of becoming not only inexpressive but un*im*pressive, and perhaps dry and pedantic. Between the two dangers, of ugliness and vulgarity on the one hand, and of aimless tone-spinning on the other, it may be that expressionism has its birth.

For something must prompt feeling, must stir the composer to his task. With the great composer, at the right time, any tone or brief motive will find an ardent response and will be sufficient to start the creative flow. But with lesser composers, and with all composers at some times, tones and tonal lines may be without appeal—and may be destitute of any distinctive affective colorings that would impel him to direct them anywhere. At such moments—and artists who deal with words and lines and pigments have similar experiences—*characteristic color* comes as a boon. Tones that were neutral of meaning and consequently of any propulsive power, assume color and gather energy if "twilight," "the fountain," "a hero," "the Hebrides," enters the mind. But once the composer gains thus a suggestion that will give his initial theme impulse and a distinctive outline, he will, if musically powerful, dismiss further concrete reportorial details from his mind, and dwell with the musical forms so generated. Should he, instead, pursue the concrete and tangible persistently, we should rightly suspect him of feebleness, not in point of visual or dramatic imagination, but certainly in point of musical imagination. And this leads us to a momentary digression. It is pathetic to find composers of divers sorts of programmatic and descriptive music given credit for the possession of imagination, and to find their music classified as "imaginative," and then be obliged to reflect that, by inference, Bach would have to be classed as unimaginative! Surely not the realists, who turn again and again to their subject for further promptings, but those who call forms into being out of an intangible realm, are the true Titans of imagination.

An artistic criterion

Notwithstanding what has been said, music may lean heavily and closely on associated interests and still be not only finely artistic but be beautiful as music. Schubert's *Erl-King,* and almost any part of a Wagnerian music-drama, illustrate the point perfectly; and in the domain of instrumental music such examples as *Danse Macabre,* and *Ein Heldenleben,* as well as most modern orchestral works, come to mind. Such compositions may be, through purely musical values, wholly acceptable as music; or they may represent, as all song does, and as Wagner believed all music should, a hybrid art, that is not necessarily a lesser art because it is not purely musical, but is certainly a different art. Whenever an art-work thus gains some part of its effect by calling up other and associated interests, it may reasonably be expected to conform to one criterion, namely, that the associations be aesthetically congruous and fusible with the aesthetic appeal of the primary art. We may not believe that associations should play so important a part as Reid [1] appears willing to assign them, but his statement of the nature of their relation to the central work is well put in these words: "In aesthetic experience there is always both a focus *and* a margin. [This] has not always been realised by the purists and formalists, by those for whom all associated meanings are anathema. The trouble is that such purists take 'association' to mean aesthetically *un*-fused,

---

[1] *A Study in Aesthetics:* Louis Arnaud Reid.

or irrelevant, association, and in their very right desire to avoid admitting these into aesthetic experience they deny the effect of association altogether, and in so doing denude their focal objects of a very large part (though not all) of their aesthetic meaning."

Well, it is true that the *Hallelujah Chorus* from *The Messiah,* as an unnamed and unknown piece of music sung in an unknown tongue, would not arouse the emotions that gather about the story of the Nativity and the deepest dreams and aspirations of mankind connected therewith. But in this example, and in all good song and all good oratorio, the aesthetic fusion *is* present. It is present in much opera, also, although text, costumes, or scenery sometimes clash with music (which can never be absurd) and arouse a sense of the ludicrous. It is present in the *Ride of the Valkyrie,* although it almost fails at a few other points in *The Ring.* To many it quite fails whenever music, which has, as Langhans says, "no prototype or corrective in the visible world surrounding us," and therefore consorts ill with material existence, calls into its court ugly, imitative sounds, and characters and incidents that reflect emotional states that would not and could not by any possibility ever express themselves in music.

Effects of musical discourse

In examining some effects of design that may be comparatively overlooked, the effects of form in extension were neglected, and the discussion of them that their nature and importance makes imperative was shifted from its logical place after *material* to this later point.

The effect of material as we have seen, is directly upon the senses. Form, as found in small units of design, was said to have a similar immediate effect. But while an extended form may conceivably be analyzed into a series of small designs, it would be a mistake to suppose that the effect of a long composition is simply a prolonged succession of these small effects. For besides senses that may be pleased, we have also memory; and the mind, through memory, is incapable of receiving the present impression as isolated, but instead relates it to the impressions that have passed, to form an event that acquires unity and extent according to the reach and fidelity of the memory. Form, therefore, is apprehended by the mind; and the characteristics it must possess to give the mind aesthetic delight become a subject either for aesthetic discussion, or, from the objective point of view, a subject for musical criticism. In both fields form is the supreme subject: for while sensuous enjoyment (to look at the matter from the standpoint of aesthetics alone) is primordial, it is still not the highest enjoyment we may experience; and response to emotionally expressive quality, though it be the most poignant, is yet far from representing the purest and most incorruptible joy possible to our spirits.

Form attains its commanding position, then, because it engages powers that are at once more extensive than the sensory and more transcendental than the expressive. The quality of a tone is a present sensation, and associated interests, such as we connected with music of the type we designated as expressive, may concern us intimately, in imagination or vicariously, as bearing on the incidents of our lives. But no possible "human interest" attaches to the piling up of tonal ideas and thoughts to the impressive climax, for instance, of a giant fugue. The delight it gives derives essentially neither from sensation (although sensation reinforces it) nor from dramatic allusions to life. The impression we actually receive is, rather, that we are following spirits of tone that, remote from earth, move through ecstasies, transports, visions, determinations, purposes, dreams, regrets and triumphs, that know no material ground and have no selfish end, but that yet are of transcendent importance and significance. The action is as though it were among the gods, and high above the clouds. When it is at its greatest, we are spellbound, are caught up from earth and its little preoccupations into a realm of passionless passion, of intense feeling that does not sear. At such times, to connect the drama with our own physical world of sharp emotional vicissitudes would be to experience a descent to a plane on which the smell of soil and the clang of earth's activities would again begin to assail our senses. Who that has witnessed a battle among the gods would descend to a street fight?

Some such contrast and sense of degradation has come to all of us when, at the close of an aesthetic experience that has left us in the clouds, we have left the hall "walking on air," and have emerged into clanging streets filled with bustling humanity intent on small enterprises. Then we have felt our horizon shrink and our lately expanded spirits contract. Only when we were halfway home could we again bend our reluctant minds to thought of the order at the grocer's; but for days after we nevertheless could not forget that once we were of greater stature.[1]

The musical basis

Extended form is capable of such effect as we have described, which is so superior to sensory effect or to poignant "emotions of life," because, unlike life, its motion is balanced, its harsh discords are resolved, its strivings are fulfilled. Life may awaken poignant feeling that knows no healing touch, and that so may drive, sway, bend, or break us. But in art, precisely because art is ideal form, because it is animation, thought, feeling, purpose, in symmetry, balance, and proportion we find our feeling stimulated and lifted to unwonted heights without that disturbing sense of ill-balance and loss of poise that clings to our keen emotional experiences in life—even when these latter are experiences of great happiness. Every great art work thus stimulates without perturbing feeling. In music, as all devotees of music know, the balances are provided in rhythms, in *tempi*, in melodic contours and undulations, in harmonic yearnings and ensuing satisfactions, in shifting

[1] Dr. Max Schoen, whose book, *Art and Beauty*, is commended to the reader, in one of his writings on aesthetics quotes Edna St. Vincent Millay's poem, *The Concert*, as an expression of aesthetic response to music. It says in beautiful verse what is attempted here in prose.

tone-colors and dynamic shadings. Every note, every item of all these factors, is there not for itself but for its relevancy; and in every good composition this relevancy is so great, the appositeness is so perfect, that the details often appear not merely as delightful but as inevitable. By that word we testify that in musical art the expectations aroused are satisfied, the yearnings stilled, the ardently adventuring tones brought to their sure haven. But this we know only in so far as our minds can span the adventure from its beginning to its end, with grasp meanwhile of the rich incidents upon the way. Otherwise the tonal stream is but a torrent of rushing sounds, undistinguished and unorganized; and while some pleasure may yet be gained therefrom, because of the sensory effects of tones and tone colors, or some poignant feelings may be elicited by programmatic interpretations that stir other interests, the sublimity of feeling that rises from the vision of ideal architectonics, of "palaces not made by hands," is left unawakened.

Two contrasting theories

Before closing this section a view of musical aesthetics that will later hold considerable practical value for us will be discussed. It offers two contrasting theories of the origin, nature and function of music: and it is not too much to say that many of the divergent trends in musical faith and preference that are disclosed by various persons with respect to their musical interests may be analyzed and clarified on the basis so provided.

The outstanding exponent of the one theory, which we may term that of the "primal cry," is, of course, Richard Wagner. According to Wagner music is essentially emotional speech. The cries of birds and animals, and of primitive men before the days of articulate speech, arose through the feeling of the utterer and were intuitively understood by the *feeling* of the hearer. This emotional speech, as used by primitive man, consisted of vowel sounds; and for its purpose it was a clear language of no small degree of efficacy. Thus, to introduce an illustration *not* given by Wagner, a savage could run into the camp of his fellows and, by his inarticulate cries, communicate to them terror, joy, or whatever emotion was dominant in him. Beyond intelligible address to feeling, however, such tone-speech could not go. In order to address the intellect objective specification became necessary. To pursue our illustration, the savage could communicate terror by his tonal cries, but if he sought to inform his fellows what it was that excited his terror he would be under the necessity of adding consonants to his speech. Or, as Wagner states it:[1] "In pure Tone-speech, with its tale of the received impression, the Feeling gave only *itself* to be understood; and this, supported by the gestures, it was quite competent to do, through its countless raisings and sinkings, prolongings and abridgings, intensifyings and abatings of the open sounds. To denote and distinguish between outer objects themselves, however, the Feeling must cast about it for something answering-to and

[1] *Opera and Drama:* Richard Wagner. Translation by W. Ashton Ellis.

embodying the impression of the object, for a distinctive garment wherewith to clothe the open tone. . . . This garment it wove from dumb articulations, which it fitted on to the open sound as a prefix or suffix, or even as both together."

But language, coming thus to address the Understanding, eventually lost its association with feeling, and was no longer a vehicle for the poet's expression. Man "pieced" his "speech-roots" together and "marred them past all knowledge by evaporating the ring of their sounding vowels to the hasty clang of Talk." [1] Music, by its prolongation of the vowels, which are the colorful and emotional element in language, must restore to it the expressive and poetic power it had lost, and give again to the poet a tone-speech by which he can voice the purely-human.

From such a beginning it is evident that the essential features of the Wagnerian music-drama may be evolved. It must be observed, however, that Wagner uses the idea to support music-drama rather than music. Nevertheless, Wagner did maintain, that music was rightly an art of expression, and that it forsook its true path whenever it pleaded for attention on the basis of its purely musical graces; and we are justified, therefore, in applying the foregoing theory to the nature and function of music in general.

If we summarize and extend the theory, we come to an explanation of music somewhat as follows:

[1] Wagner: *op. cit.*

1. The first facts in music are emotional cries, as of birds, animals, primitive men.

2. In origin music is characteristically vocal.

3. The individual, at the moment of musical experience, is strongly active (emotionally).

4. The value of music to humanity is to heighten man's power by vast intensification of feeling.

5. The highest temple of musical art would be the music-drama auditorium.

In contrast to this general view—a view that is seldom if ever, explicitly stated, but that may be discerned as implied by attitudes and preferences—is another, similarly existing by implication only. It assumes that music arose because of the Pleasure of the Ear in Tone. Instead of the emotional cries of birds, animals and men, this theory would find the origin of music in the twang of the bow-string, the sound of the wind in the reeds, the murmur of falling waters, the ring of wood on wood. All natural sonorities would become primary experiences in man's musical development. As against the other view, we would now think of music as primarily or characteristically instrumental; would conceive the individual, at the moment of musical experience, not as being strongly active but as being sensitively and beautifully receptive; would find the value of music to humanity to reside (in a word) in culture—that is, in the ability to find joy in every beauty that nature or man provided; and would find the true temple of music represented, not by the

operatic stage, but perhaps by the organ-loft in St. Thomas
Church in Leipzig, as Bach communed with incorporeal
visions; or perhaps by the small chamber in which a string
quartet would seek glories from an unseen world.

It would be wrong to assume hastily that these two
theories represent only the well known points of view of
the singer as compared with the instrumentalist. The matter
is far more complicated than that. Many instrumentalists,
judged by repertory and style of playing, would have to be
identified with the "primal-cry" theory, and many *lieder*
singers, as well as other vocalists whom we shall discover
later, by the same signs must be judged as holding to the
tenets of the Pleasure-of-the-Ear-in-Tone theory. The two
outlooks, indeed, are inextricably interwoven and are often
wholly fused. It is enough now to know each, and to feel
assured that we have a criterion by which certain values that
we shall wish to appraise in the pages to come can be
rather confidently evaluated.

PSYCHOLOGICAL BEARINGS

Chapter Seven

The Young Child's Responses to Music and Song

Sensation and perception in the child

While we agree that the child, at the age of five or six years, lives largely in a world of sensory experience, we may have failed at times to draw the right deductions from that general principle. It may be, even, that the nature and effect of sensory experience itself have not been carefully defined, and that our practices have accordingly rested upon a vague and hastily accepted assumption.

Under the "intellectual climate" that has prevailed—and again we must thank James Truslow Adams for the term—it has been assumed, in practice, if not in creed, that any object presented to the child is perceived "objectively." In other words, much of education, in music as in other subjects, has rested, if we can trust appearances, upon the belief that the child's characteristic mode of attention is the perceptive rather than the intuitive. Now we would not deny, since a child must learn to direct his life in a practical, physical world, that this rationalistic or factual aspect of it should be brought to his attention, and that knowledges and skills on his part that are necessary to his dealings with matter should be developed. On the other hand, it is surely a grave error to ignore the fact, as psychological thought has largely done, that every sensation and percept has a subjective side as well as an objective one, and that every sensation and percept is not only received but is referred to a sentient something back of the percept, that accepts it in terms of interests, preferences, and purposes that work toward that "coordinated maintenance" of personality of which Haldane spoke. In short, a percept, with any of us, is accepted (or rejected) in terms of subjective alimentation, if we may use the expression; which is to say, that it has flavor, meaning, significance, as a *present subjective experience that ministers to subjective needs and interests,* quite apart from its value as a factor of utility in our encounters with material and rational conditions and problems.

Aesthetic quality of responses

It must be obvious, since such response as we have described is in terms of acceptability and value, that it is essentially of the nature of aesthetic response. The feeling of like or dislike, of being drawn or repelled, of interest or indifference, is a selection in terms of absorption, divination, and feeling, however weak, subconscious, and diffused the feeling may be. Especially is this true in the case of the child; and it seems almost incredible, in view of the obviousness of that fact, that so little attention has been given it either in educational theory or practice. For it must be evident that the child, lacking the shrewd experience in dealing with things in terms of practical advantage that is acquired by the adult, must approach his world on a basis of present affective reaction. This propensity, indeed, constitutes at once his simplicity, his ingenuousness, and that impractical innocence and lack of judgment from the effects of which he must be protected, and out of which he must be educated. But on the other hand, to be blind to the worth of this affective and aesthetic life, to fail to see in it the germ from which taste, discrimination, ideals, and character must be developed, is a tragic blunder. The capacity to understand, sympathize and enjoy, in forgetfulness of self and absorption in the object, is implicit in this capacity. In such light the observation that children are the true artists is seen to be not a mere piece of sentimentality but the deliberate statement of a truth. That they are not always artists, that they live at times in an almost animal world, and at times must be guided to live in a very calculating world, is beside the point. Adult artists must also live as practical men. No one contends, anyway, that all of life can or should be lived on the aesthetic plane. The contention is rather that it should not all be lived on the plane of rational utilitarianism. And to ensure escape from this latter fate, which lately has appeared as an uncomfortably near danger, it is urged at this point that in sensation and perception, *especially in the child,* we recognize a feeling side as well as a knowing side, an aesthetic as well as a rational response.

When we realize that sensation and perception are not

necessarily for the sake of knowledge that will prompt action toward proximate ends, but may claim value because they give nurture that will build toward broad and far-off ends, the nature of that which we bring to the child to sense and perceive will be judged in very different terms. To the child in the kindergarten and first grade we bring music. If we assume that knowledge and practical power are, or should be, his interest, we will bring him staff notation and techniques. If we assume that concrete life-situations interest him—and they do; *but not musically*—we will bring him song-texts of more or less literal character, and of less or more poetic quality, and hang these on questionable tunes that owe their dubious nature to the fact that they were regarded as subsidiary to the main purpose anyway. Or we may, if our pedagogical ambition soars and our high determination will not be balked, introduce him, through one medium or another, to works of the masters, that he may early grow to recognize and (it may be) love them.

But perhaps, instead of any of these, we may recall that a child is in a sensory stage; that a bright-eyed but hard-surfaced objective focus of attention is not more normal to him than is a wondering drinking-in of sensations that absorb him; and that development of the germ of musicalness that is in him, if we can possibly find any way to effect it, is our task. In that case we may reflect that since his attention-span is brief, and his ability to coordinate and integrate is slight, any very long composition will necessarily become a series of detached impressions rather than a unitary whole, and will consequently be foreign to any powers of musical judgment he may have. We will realize, further, that the activity of his sensory powers is likely to conflict with his ability to attend to expressive or programmatic meanings, and that he probably hears, even at times to our undoing, simply what comes into his ears. Moreover, the moods and meanings of most expressive music arise out of thoughts and states of feeling that reflect maturity, not childhood; and unless they have been deliberately chosen to appeal to supposed juvenile "interests" (in which case they are likely to be farcical and to introduce associations that do not "fuse" aesthetically with music) they are, as were long compositions, alien to the child's range of response.

Song in relation to children

But songs must constitute the basis of approach, and all song contains in its texts some measure of associated or programmatic interest. That interest, however, may be extremely slight without in the least impairing the child's interest in the song as music and rhythm. Indeed, in the pleasure children and primitive people take in singing meaningless words, or countless repetitions of a few words that soon lose all literal meaning, and again in their tendency to ignore the "expressive" meaning of texts by reciting verses in "sing-song" fashion, or by singing songs in obedience to rhythmic and melodic implications rather than in obedience to lingual meanings, we find clear evidence of the possibilities for aesthetic delight that reside in these impersonal factors alone. Often, in fact, the greater delight may be ensured by careful avoidance, in the case of young children, of texts that bring them too sharply in contact with a literal world that they do not seek and that may even appear disquieting or formidable to them. At the very least, any associations suggested by texts should be both germane to childhood and, moreover, should be of such character that they fuse, as associations in all song-texts should do, not only with the aesthetic character *of the particular song melody,* but with the aesthetic nature of *music* itself. And this distinction is important. "Expression" in song is all too frequently supposed to consist, if we may judge by what is heard, in an obtrusive or coloristic emphasis upon a word or line here and there. The result is that thought and feeling are abruptly swerved into channels that are incongruous with the essential spirit of music and with the integrity of the particular piece of music, as a whole. That the particular melody, at the particular moment, may lend itself to such departure and may even invite it, only proves that the composer, as well as a singer, was aesthetically obtuse. Were such a "local-color" system correct, dramatic prose and an elocutionist would provide all the necessary agencies for a concert.

Nevertheless, song at its best is an art-mixture, and although it is a simple one it will still disclose some characteristic features of such mixtures. In their greater complexity, as in opera, these mixtures are likely to assail mind and senses with aesthetic appeals of such disparate nature that they neutralize rather than enhance one another, and the result of their collective impact may thus be an effect that is inferior, in purity and depth, to that attainable by any one of the factors separately. If consummate artistry, as with Wagner, succeeds in balancing and welding the different arts beautifully, we have, as Wagner declared, a new art that, as a unified art-form, makes a new kind of appeal to our receptivity and that must be judged by the symmetries and balances attained within its own complex self. Naturally, attainment of symmetrical proportion becomes more difficult as complexity increases, and the weak creative artist incurs formidable dangers when he makes such attempts. The hearer (or spectator) may also find difficulty in assimilating so much at once. Even in the simpler mixture, song, we find adults comparatively undiscriminating, because the interest of words submerges ordinary sensibilities to music, with the result that hearers tolerate imperfections in both composition and performance that would soon arouse distaste were the same song, for instance, played instrumentally. And if this be true of adults it is, of course, more true of children, because these latter require still greater simplicity and unity if they are not to be thrown into confusion. It follows, then, that only when songs for children are short, have words that consort beautifully with the ideal nature of music, and when they are properly presented—that is to say, words and music wholly blended or fused at the outset—can a genuine education in music (and not in feelings or manners or morals, to a meagre accompaniment of music) be begun upon the basis of songs alone.

Attractiveness of tonal elements

The requisite fusion, when music (and not language) is the subject of instruction, must be a fusion of words with music and not a fusion of music with words. The first preoccupation of the child, in so far as a musical atmosphere is considered desirable, must, in other words, be with the musical element. To induce such preoccupation is astonishingly easy; and the feasibility is due precisely to the capacity of the child for intuitive or aesthetic attention to all engaging sensations. Such an engaging sensation is musical *tone*. Like prismatic colors to his eye, it comes to his ear as the most satisfying sensation that can ever break into his consciousness through that organ of sense. No other noises or sounds are ever equally pleasant. A child hardly old enough to stand, and hardly tall enough when standing to reach a piano keyboard, will therefore remain for long minutes pressing down the keys—and perhaps the same key—again and again, indulging his aesthetic response to tone, and also deriving the same keen pleasure from thus exercising and developing one of his senses that he derives from exercising his body. Bells, the liquid note of a bird, the klangs and klings, sonorous and thin, that come to him from wood, metal, glass, and other vibrant sources, and the sound of his own voice, used "instrumentally" and not for emotional or articulate expression, in croonings, hummings, cries, and yodels—these all preoccupy and fascinate him similarly. There is clear indication in all this, could the signs but be read aright, of the path that his early musical education should follow.

With respect to aesthetic development the path indicated, which is first preoccupation with tone, and soon with tone in designs of rhythmic and melodic outline, is as promising as it is with respect to psychological indications. The emphasis placed upon this point in an earlier chapter is probably not forgotten, but Santayana's clear statement, "The beauty of material is thus the groundwork of all higher beauty," may be recalled now as having new significance. To the beauty of material—tone—we find the child extremely sensitive. Not only is he keenly responsive to its appeal, but his discrimination at this time with respect to all of its characteristics—pitch, power, quality, color—is exceedingly delicate. The investigations of Dr. Seashore [1] appear to have proven conclusively that musical discrimination remains fixed throughout life. It remains true, however, that *attention to* the sensations of tone that one receives may greatly increase one's power to deal with tones—as all teachers of "ear-training" have observed. In relation to our present point it is true also that the child, not having learned to *exclude* what he does not wish to attend to—a power that is at the very base of all learning, else we should all be as helpless as a camera when we turned our eyes upon the world—hears with a literalness that is akin to a phono-

[1] *The Psychology of Musical Talent:* Carl Emil Seashore.

graphic recording plate. Moreover, his senses are not indurated to receive shocks of such strength as those which older persons can absorb with equanimity. As the skin of a child differs, in being more delicate of texture and more sensitive than that of an older person, so do his ears differ with respect to the volume and purity of tone that they can receive with pleasure. Children may be observed to clap their hands to their ears at a *sforzando* from the percussions and brasses of an orchestra, and to fall into excited merriment at the emotional *fortissimo* singing of an operatic *prima donna*. Mother's voice in a lullaby, the tones of a harp as contrasted with a concert grand piano, a flute as compared with a trumpet, are much nearer the child's aesthetic range. We must not be misled by the fact that children also like noise; for they seek noise for physical and mental excitement rather than for what we think of as aesthetic pleasure. Moreover, their taste for the one is not more pronounced (although it is naturally more noticeable) than is their taste for the other.

It follows, then, that dealings with tone *as tone* will not be without interest to the child; that in such dealings he will be developing the basic aesthetic sense that is the necessary "groundwork" for all higher aesthetic response to music; that his aptitude for such dealings is very high, being characterized by a delicacy, a microscopic quality of hearing, that enables him to discriminate sensitively between small shades of purity and impurity, loudness and softness, timbre, and pitch; and that an innocent and unspoiled literalness of hearing provides in him a bulwark against insincerity and false tendencies that can only be broken down by the most persistent blandishments of a misguided teacher.

The Place of Rhythm

The fact that we have so far said little about rhythm does not imply that we consider it unimportant, but rather that it is here viewed from a somewhat unusual standpoint. In later chapters we shall more than once come upon rhythm as operative in our aesthetic and pedagogical theory and practice. We shall not, however, inquire into its origin and nature as a separate phenomenon; and the reasons for such a decision are all that need be set forth here.

While rhythm is a salient and important factor in music, it is not the distinguishing mark of music. Verse, the dance, walking, the procession of the seasons, the graphic arts, indeed, almost the whole of nature's processes and of man's activities and productions, reveal the presence of rhythm. It is truly a universal element. On the other hand, that which music possesses that is shared by none of the other arts, and which gives it its distinctive character and peculiar value, is tone. That is to say, tone and tones, devoid of rhythm, as produced, for example, by an Aeolian harp, will exert that charm and have that particular kind of aesthetic effect that is characteristic of music. In comparison, rhythm detached from tone, as in the ticking of a metronome or the clapping of hands, may have effect, it is true, but not effect of the kind that is characteristic of music. Such rhythm may, indeed, be wholly without address to the ear, as in flashes from a lighthouse, or in silent movements of the body.

But rhythm is indispensable to music if the latter is to have extent and is to command the continuity and absorption of attention that are essential to any but the most rudimentary aesthetic experience. The tone of the Aeolian harp, however potent its charm, can not hold us long. Movement in time, organized by periodicities and recurrences—which latter, in themselves, represent periodicities—is necessary. Nevertheless, although the form is of rhythm, the substance is of tone; and in directing a child's approach to the very heart of music, the desirable order—although the statement is subject to considerable qualification—is therefore from tone to rhythm, rather than from rhythm to tone.

While rhythm, separated from tone, does not have the effect characteristic of music, it undeniably does have some effect, and very potent and important effect. In a broad sense of the term, that effect is aesthetic; but if the connotation be restricted, the term may appear less applicable. Perhaps instead of the words "aesthetic effect" we should substitute the words "effect of beauty." The problem will then appear clarified. From this point of view we may see that the effect of the Aeolian harp is to arouse, in however rudimentary form, the sense of beauty; but it is questionable whether the effect of rhythm without tone, however potent and stirring the example, can be said to be that of arousing the sense of beauty. For characteristically beauty absorbs us in contemplation. We are drawn up and out of ourselves by it. In contrast, rhythm, especially as organized in non-resonant sounds, enters into us and makes us more conscious of ourselves and of our individuality, as set off against all else in the universe. Rhythm, indeed, appears to be broadly physiological rather than aural, and to seek a welcome in the body rather than a haunt in the realm of ideas. It has power and value, but not of the kind that we associate with beauty. Detached from music it never gains the grace, the flexibility, the infinite variety, that it gathers in association with music. When it weds beauty, it acquires loveliness, and beauty gathers power. In eurhythmics we see such a marriage. In the primary grades of a school, *in the music lesson,* we shall therefore not seek rhythm too insistently, in its single state, lest we find it undeveloped and unkempt, and never thereafter learn to know its lovelier self; and again, we shall not try to isolate it lest its stronger voice, if heard alone, may cause us to hear too faintly the purer voice of music that tries to sing above the rhythmic joinery. Rather we shall regard it as a form which music, in its own growth, bodies forth,[1] just as a tree grows into or creates its own distinctive form. And so viewed it becomes a beautiful raiment, inseparable from the lovely body that it clothes.

[1] See Chapter Six, *Phrasing,* in *The Eloquent Baton:* Earhart. Also see Chapter IV, *On Rhythm,* in *Music to the Listening Ear:* Earhart.

Chapter Eight

Musical Responses in Relation to Musical Materials

In the preceding chapter it was implied, rather than stated, that the child, so far as vocal music is concerned, should begin with practice on tonal calls and with brief songs, and should use his voice in these as a musical instrument to address and please the ear, rather than as an organ of articulate speech to address and inform the intellect. Without entering into a discussion of methods and material in detail, which would be out of place in this book, some corollaries should be drawn from the foregoing propositions.

Musical worth and educational worth

No one will deny that all musical material used in the education of children should have the highest possible degree of merit as music. When we assert this we feel that we are on very solid ground, and that we have a criterion which we can use with greatest confidence in making selections of all necessary musical materials. It would be a pity to shake that confidence; but on the other hand it appears imperative to safeguard it from the perils that will follow if such a broad generalization is hastily and blindly followed.

The first distinction to be made is obvious, and probably has come before the thought of every teacher of music. It is that educational worth and musical worth are not in any fixed proportion. The more worthy of two pieces of music may be too long, or too mature, or too difficult, to make it acceptable educationally. This problem is complicated in song by the presence of words. Few teachers, however, fail to select texts that are within the range of the child's vocabulary and experience. Here, indeed, they may go too far, and in the search for texts that are juvenile are likely to select some that are trivial and that are moreover wholly incompatible with the spirit of music. But disregarding the problem of texts, and assuming that the problem is settled in a satisfactory manner, there still remain problems of appropriateness with respect to melody. A good melody, even of folk-song type, and although it is brief and within the child's vocal range, may express a maturity of mood that is out of keeping with the *timbre* of the child's voice, and probably is correlatively out of keeping with his affective disposition. Or it may lack the simplicity and transparency of form, as inherent in short phrases, recurrences and sequences, and uniformity in rhythmic movement, that would give it hold in his mind. The number of really superior songs remaining after all of these limitations, and others that appear later in connection with sight-singing, are heeded, is likely to be considerably reduced: and the teacher is then confronted with the problem of using songs that *comparatively,* at least, are inferior.

But two considerations here modify the aspect of the general principle. The first is that superiority, if sought with inflexible determination, must yield finally only a few choice examples of perfection. The apex of the pyramid tends to become a vanishing point. So has the slow verdict of time thrust to the top, for example, the odd-numbered Beethoven symphonies, the *Pilgrim's Chorus* from *Tannhäuser,* and other fulfilled aspirations of compositional endeavor. But no one would contend that the development of a musician would be comparatively retarded if he played any compositions less perfect than these. There is a point below which he may not pass without danger; but on the other hand there is a saving grace that will carry him through much that is *comparatively* inferior, and that may be well adapted to one stage or another of his progress, without any damage whatever to his artistic development. This saving grace is his own attitude toward *everything* he performs. Sincerity, the "last full measure of devotion" toward making the product as beautiful as it can be made, will not alter the rank of the composition *as an art-work,* but it *will* alter profoundly the value of the exercise, as an educational or developmental experience in the artistic life of the performer. Thus Toscanini astonishes, perhaps perturbs, his admirers by placing Rossini's overture to *Semiramide* on one of his programs; but to the playing of that somewhat commonplace composition he brings such a wealth of artistic power that the hearing of it becomes a lesson in artistic musical values.

Musical beauty and beautiful music

And this brings us to an observation that has not, perhaps, been sufficiently weighed. The path that leads to the land of aesthetic musical delight and understanding is not defined and safeguarded wholly in terms of acquaintance and experience with a repertory of standard compositions. Apart from the features that give any composition its distinctive place and rank among the myriad that exist, are factors that are necessary to any and all music if it would become distinguished from mere ugly noise. These elemental attributes we have tried to define in Chapter Six, with particular emphasis upon *tone* as the distinctive possession of music. Now we would add that for purposes of education toward appreciation it is far more important to develop sensitivity toward these pervasive and basic constituents of all music than it is to focus attention upon the distinctive features of one composition as compared with another. In fact, the latter procedure is backward; for it must be evident that if one does not know or respond to the factors in music that make it music at all, he is illy prepared to enjoy and discriminate between musical compositions; and this is with respect both to the intrinsic value of compositions *as* compositions, and also with respect to musical values as the pieces are *heard in performance*.

On the other hand, if one does know, and is keenly responsive to, the factors that constitute music in general, he is then prepared to enjoy the specific modes of employment of these factors that are represented in many compositions of different types. The material presented to young children therefore does not represent repertory so much as it represents their introduction to tone, rhythm, color, form, design; and while no one would deny the value inherent in good music, especially when used to give an experience that will subconsciously form taste and provide a basis for later studies, it is a grievous mistake to focus attention preponderantly or wholly upon compositional values and disregard at the same time the values that make up the very stuff of which the compositions are made.

The presence of such error is disclosed in courses in music appreciation that present good compositions in a poor or ugly tonal investiture, or in courses in rote singing that employ excellent songs but permit of somewhat graceless singing, while at the same time the musical, national, expressive or historical values of the songs are proclaimed. Later results of the error may be found in hypocritical composition-worship, in pianists who play good music gracelessly, and in concert audiences that applaud a name but show small critical judgment either as to the worth of compositions or the qualities of performance. The endeavor appears to be, when teachers err in the way described, to grasp a far goal that has been forecast, without discerning the steps by which that goal may be approached.

The remedy will spring from the understanding that the goal is not distant but present, and must be reached in each momentary endeavor; and that is to say that there are joys and values that lie on every hand, in material that is almost everywhere available, and that those values are simply the aesthetic values that lie in the elements that constitute anything that may be called music.

Proportioning values: an aid to criticism

The teacher may gain some additional aid toward directing practice, both with young children and older ones, by reflecting upon some illustrations of the balancing of musical and compositional values that come within everyone's experience. Making a rough generalization, it may be said that music may sound much better than it is, or may be much better than it sounds. The statement is apparently based wholly upon the thought of performance. Our major concern, however, is the attitude of the performer, and more specifically with his progress in musical understanding according to the direction given his attention toward the one or the other of the two interests between which we have discriminated.

Great singers afford us excellent illustrations of artistic devotion bestowed upon comparatively poor material, because the literature for the principal solo instruments contains few compositions as brief, simple, and sometimes commonplace, as are the slighter compositions in the literature of song. Yet who has not experienced delight—and delight, let us say, on purely musical grounds—from hearing some great artist sing, perhaps as an encore, some favorite song of most modest musical pretensions? Most of us have heard songs for which, as musicians, we have small respect, thus lifted to the plane of an aesthetic achievement. If we analyze the factors that contribute to the result we find beautiful tone, perfect intonation (else there could not have been musical delight), lovely nuance, perfect lifting and lovely relinquishment of each phrase. But none of these are compositional qualities; they are elements of music—of any and all music—that in themselves are aesthetic materials. Given devotion to them, the artist may function as artist, and the appreciative hearer may listen with pleasure, notwithstanding the art-work is of humble rank.

On the other hand, who of us has not suffered from hearing a masterpiece of song sung with a poor quality of voice, and with false intonations and unmusicianly phrasing? And with relation to the child and to his musical education, which of the two experiences would be the more desirable? Perhaps we should conclude that it would be the one that gave him the most of immediate aesthetic delight. And since the child is in a sensory stage, and is less able to appreciate either compositional strengths or expressive meanings than he is to appreciate simple aesthetic elements, choice would probably fall upon the first of the two cases.

Other illustrations abound, but the point need not be labored. The success of a widely known American orchestra that confines itself almost wholly to a repertory of jazz and other popular types of music, is almost certainly due to the fact that it gives to empty thought a specious loveliness that is compounded of the primitive yet basic aesthetic elements that we have described. In fact, a road to popularity is to bewitch the senses while asking little of the mind. If to sensuous and formal beauty we add expressive interest, the number of combinations is considerably increased. Thus we may have, as in the last case cited, sensuous beauty and formal worthlessness; or we may have sensuous ugliness and formal beauty (often the over-ambitious neophyte's contribution); sensuous ugliness and expressive interest; both sensuous ugliness and formal weakness but great expressive excitement (the vulgar "descriptive" piece); or both sensuous and formal beauty plus great impressive or expressive appeal. One restraining influence, however, works against combining factors that in point of excellence are at opposite ends of the scale. It is that there are compatibilities that are recognized by the most obtuse sensibilities. Just as no sculptor, for instance, would invest his noblest conception in ugly, mottled clay, but would demand marble, or as a composer could not confide a heavenly melody to a metallic, jangling piano, so the lesser artist that is in every man shrinks from combining a beautiful thought with an ugly sensuous medium. Or we might put it negatively, and say that there are compatibilities in ugliness, and that no one is offended when a vulgar thought is given expression through an ugly medium. Thus no one is offended when a vulgar and inane jazz tune is played on a tinny and out-of-tune piano, or by a noisy, jazzy orchestra. All is quite concordant, for vulgarity is mated with vulgarity. The medium is all that the tune deserves, and is, in fact, invited by the tune; else why are the players led to squall through muted trumpets, grunt through trombones, and squawk through constricted saxophones? Indeed, it may be charitably reckoned as artistic discernment that leads them thus to adapt the vehicle of expression to the thought to be expressed.

Practical applications

It is refreshing to turn back to the purity and sensibility of childhood. With his small but pure voice, which is fitted to express little but idyllic meanings, with his sensitive ears, with his slight interest in, or capacity to express artistically through his voice, the strong emotions of expressive music, and with tendency to preoccupy himself with the sensuous factors of musical appeal, the child comes to us to receive musical development at our hands. We must exercise his voice and his hearing in strictest association. He must sing words as well as tones, and his songs must be adapted to his interest, his understanding, and his abilities for musical expression. They must be the best songs possible within these limitations. The purpose of these latter pages is to direct thought to the possibility that some appropriate and fruitful contributions to his development may be lost if too inflexible attention is given to compositional value alone. What the child seeks in performance, in terms of general musical effect, is quite as important, and will be quite as influential in results, as will the intrinsic value of the composition to which he gives more or less beautiful expression.

Chapter Nine

Developing Musical Power

If the young child, as we have argued, has a tendency to respond in affective or aesthetic terms to that which crowds upon his senses, he is disposed to feel or *see into,* rather than *learn about;* to *appreciate* (in subconscious attitudes) rather than to *know;* to become charmed, absorbed, *enthralled by* —and all of these are terms connoting the deep response we term aesthetic—rather than become *interested in* the object of attention. But while this is a tendency, and obviously one in which the promise of a right future affective development for the child is wholly predicated, it is by no means a constant and ineradicable tendency. We have intimated, indeed, that modern education has characteristically disregarded precisely this aesthetic attitude in the child, with the result that it has been inhibited, has become to some extent atrophied, and that development toward humane and cultured living has thereby been defeated. That the tendency exists, and exists in strong measure, means no more, therefore, than that a potentiality exists. That is to say, the child has within him a germ of aesthetic development, just as he has a germ of physical development and a germ of intellectual development; but this germ will not develop without nurture, any more than would the others. It is the business of teachers of music, art, and literature to provide the requisite nurture.

Gaining intuitive attention

Notwithstanding the child's predisposition toward aesthetic unselfconsciousness, together with the attractiveness of musical material itself, it is not an easy task to bring the two into that intimate communion from which musical development can proceed. Or perhaps the means are so easy that they are overlooked. In the first place the objective stir and the institutional oppressiveness of the schoolroom must be counterbalanced. They do not blend with the voice of music. The teacher, too, especially if young and inexperienced, may believe she must be dynamic. She must; but her dynamic energy must not be of a kind that dispels the dynamic power that inheres in music. The busy, physically animated, teacher, or the teacher who imposes upon the group a personal domination, even if it be of a glowing, benignant kind, becomes an opaque body thrust between the children and the shining vision of music. Rather her strength must be that of her subject; and in so far as her voice is an overtone, reflecting the preoccupation of her own mind with a musical content, and in so far as she becomes thereby an agency that, unnoticed in itself, conveys the voice of music to the children, to that extent she gains power and her charges gain understanding. The children did not see the Pied Piper; they followed the vision evoked by his pipes.

In the kindergarten a chord played upon the piano is used to still, concentrate, and unify the group; and the very character and strength of the tone influence the quality of the reaction. In the primary grades, numerous verbal directions, sometimes delivered in tones of voice that are wholly incompatible with any musical preoccupation, are likely to be substituted for the chord, even as a prelude to singing.

The wise teacher will bring music into the room at the earliest possible moment, and will prepare for its entry by doing nothing that is alien to its reception. Music, not the teacher, is the presence that is awaited. There need be no sepulchral hush, no constraint, no hypocritical sentiment, but neither should there be unseemly clangor and stir that would ostracize a presence that is pleasant and life-giving. A single tone, sounded once, is frequently all the command that is needed.

But a tone sounded must be heard, and heard not only with the physical ear but by the mind. A common error consists in asking from the class too quick a response or reproduction of what has been heard. The tone given should not in itself be too loud or too brief. If loud and brief, and particularly if followed by immediate response, that response is likely to be inaccurate, careless, and of bad vocal quality. But if the example is really exemplary, and if a moment of silence follows, the responding tone is likely to be pure, correct and floating.

Developing auditory imagery

It is necessary, then, that tones be received into the mind, and that they echo there for a time before they are again thrust into physical existence, if anything like communion with music is to be established. This is what happens when the child experiments alone at piano or otherwise with tones and tunes and sounds; but all too frequently it disappears in the schoolroom. It can be made to happen in the schoolroom, however, by many devices. Echoes, following at an interval of a second or two, are useful. Or the children may be asked to wait, after the key is given, and find whether their memories are "a half-minute long," and whether they can then give the correct tone. The teacher herself may develop her own musical memory and power of musical ideation by joining the class in trying to begin again on the pitch after a long interruption, and by refraining from sounding the pitch-pipe again, or hurrying across the room to the piano to find the pitch, after every brief halt. Such incessant tuning-up is often only a bad habit, and presup- poses a weakness that does not exist but that it rapidly serves to create.

Other devices are useful, and with older children the instruction may be greatly elaborated. Little children may be introduced to the idea of imagery by being asked whether they can remember just what mother said, and how her voice sounded when she started them to school that morn- ing; whether they can hear (in imagination) the voice of a

playmate in his call outside their window; whether they can
see the front door or the kitchen, or the dress mother wore,
now, when they are in school. In higher grades not only
are all these devices useful, but others may be added. Before the initial beat the baton may be raised very slowly, be
poised expectantly and suggestively, and the initial tone
may thus be kept ringing in all minds until the baton falls.
Or the pupils may open books, read a phrase silently, turn
books face down, and then sing. Unless pupils make such
attempts it often happens that their eyes become filled with
notes while their heads remain empty of tone. Or a pitch—
say middle C—may be given, a succession of chords be
played upon the piano, a further moment of silence be
enjoined, and then the memory-image may be evoked. This
latter device may be graded by elaborating the "erasing"
chords into a long series that, at the furthest point of development, ends in a contradictory key—say D-flat major, if
the tone set for recall were C. Curiously, in this latter case,
a response that follows too quickly upon the heels of the
last piano-chord will almost always adopt the final piano
pitch, while if an interval of silence is enjoined after the
piano has finished, the original C will gradually reassert
itself in the mind. Such a fact in itself testifies to the desirability in music training of requiring less quick sensory
response and more cerebration.

Finally, a class may be made so conscious of mental content that a long step in general understanding may result.
Thus some eighth-grade pupils, following some twenty

minutes of such exercises and discussions as have been described, were asked what they would be if all they had seen, heard, felt, since they were born, were wiped from their minds. One pupil replied, "Just a little baby"; another succinctly answered, "Nothing." The teacher, commenting, said that "nothing" was nearly right; that what they carried in their minds was really all they were; that they could fill that storehouse with ugly or beautiful, with useful or useless, memories, but that it would appear to be good sense to keep ugly, foolish, and perhaps haunting spectres of thought, from gaining place. Then the pupils, turning again to the song with which they had at first been occupied, were asked: "Where was this song before it was in the book?" They agreed it was "in somebody's head." "And where must it be before you can sing it, before it is yours to enjoy?" They answered: "In our heads." Said the teacher: "Right. You are to lift it out of the books and into your heads, where you can hold it always for your own pleasure. I thought awhile ago, before we began trying our musical memories, that you were not using your heads enough. See whether you can not remember the song now, and sing it with your books closed." The pupils were quite astonished to find that their heads held more than they had supposed. A new type of effort was started, the song was soon sung from memory, and the singing was more beautiful than it would ever have been had they sung from the books while "their eyes were full of notes." Their musical minds had at

first simply been idling while other powers worked list-
lessly and ineffectively.

Music as a subjective art

Such discussion of practical detail as the foregoing would
be out of place in this book were it not necessary to emphasize strongly the peculiar nature of the "attention" and
"thought" that make for the development of real musical
power. The substance of such thought is *music itself;* and
not music as a present physical sensation, but music as idea,
as remembered, as speaking in the mind. There, indeed,
is its birthplace and characteristically its home. Langhans,[1]
in describing it, speaks of "the incorporeity of its material,
the quickly passing tone, and the absence of a prototype
and corrective such as the other arts possess in the visible
world surrounding us"; and he concludes that music, therefore, "is justly called the most subjective of the arts." Dr.
Burney says, less justly: "Music is the only presentative art;
all the other arts are representative." This would seem to
reduce the other arts almost to the function of imitation,
and is consequently an over-statement. Nevertheless, music
is of curiously subjective origin; and were the life of music
restricted to the moments when the lights are glowing
and the instruments are sounding, it would have a tragically
brief and barren existence. Fortunately, its continued existence is in the mind; and only there, as with any other

[1] *History of Music in Twelve Lectures:* Wilhelm Langhans; translated by J. H.
Cornell.

knowledge or power, does it become rightly fruitful in terms of human usefulness. To induce such mental acquisition and preoccupation is the work of every teacher. The artist is one whose mind is preoccupied with haunting images of line, mass, color, light, and shadow; the poet's mind must be filled with images, words, rhythms, with which he loves to deal; the musician's mind must be filled with tones, tunes, harmonies, rhythms, forms, which shape themselves again and again in his imagination, to his absorbed delight. This condition the music teacher must strive to arouse in the student.

The musician in the child

But, it will be objected, the child is not a musician. To this we may answer that in so far as we teach him music at all we must approach him as one. If he is incapable of musical memory, if he is some sort of musically responsive lower animal, such as a musical dog or mouse, that is sensitive to music while it sounds but becomes barren of a single tone when it has ceased, he is uneducable musically, and any and all effort on our part is wasted. Transient sensational entertainment is then the limit of the contribution we can make to him. It must be confessed that some vague notion of this kind appears to have lurked at times in the minds of teachers, with the result that superficial and even vulgar programs of so-called instruction have sometimes been pursued.

Assuming that the child is not musically intelligent, but

that he has, perhaps, rational intelligence, teachers of music have thus approached him from every angle except the musical one. He has been instructed in staff-notation, in musical literature, in textual meanings, or what not, while that which was specifically musical in him was left uncared for. *Direct approach to the musical power that is in the child* should rather characterize the methods of the teacher. That this musical power is slight is beside the question, and to persist on that ground is to evade the issue. In whatever degree musical power does exist, it is at least that which is to be educated (so far as the music teacher is concerned); and to educate something else because the teacher can not discern this small musical embryo, or because she can see more readily how to develop other interests and powers, is a plain dereliction. The teacher who has tended toward such error, either because of the objectivism and rationalism current in education, or because she is not herself particularly musical, is urged to reflect that every outstanding achievement in musical education or training has rested precisely upon the faith of the instructor—a faith that is practically never betrayed—in the native musical powers of the instructed, and upon a consequent direct appeal to and activation of those powers.

Specifically those powers are, we repeat, an aesthetic sensitivity to tone (the very substance of music) in all its colors, degrees of force, ranges of pitch, melodic undulations, modes of rhythmic motion, and architectonic arrangements. We repeat, also, that this sensitivity, being aesthetic and moving, is not a present sense-perception alone, but leaves a residue of auditory imagery which forms the substance of whatever musicalness there is in the child and constitutes the foundation of all his further development. To add to this stock of imagery, not only in the way of remembering pieces but also in the way of remembering general musical effects, and to promote active dealings with these, is the business of the teacher. That the degree of power possessed by the learners is small, and that their advance, measured in terms of objective conquest, is slight, is beside the point. The *kind* of growth—whether it is *in terms of music*—and not the reach of it, is the vital consideration.

We can not all have the capacity represented by Mozart's achievement when he remembered the whole of Allegri's *Miserere* on one hearing, but we can all be made happy by the possession of some degree of that capacity. The cultivation of that degree of it which we possess constitutes our musical education, and no sort of education related to music that fails in this essential development is a satisfactory substitute. Kenyon Cox [1] says that through the Middle Ages and the Renaissance "every craftsman was an artist in his degree, and every artist was but a craftsman of a superior sort." Just so may every person be a true musician in his degree; and this is better than to be a false musician in a greater degree.

[1] *Artist and Public:* Kenyon Cox.

Practical evidences of right method

When the music lesson is characterized by a musical pre-occupation that reaches beyond present aural sensation—and this may be gained by some of the measures described —little or no overt control will be required of the teacher. To listen for tones that, wraith-like, emerge from the recesses of memory, produces in itself a concentration and control that silences objective stir and restrains errant impulse. Restless, roving, eyes grow still, bodies become quiet. The tones or tunes that have lain in the mind moreover become idealized, by that strange alchemy that transmutes sensation and perception into imagery, and issue forth purified of the grossness and imperfections inherent in the physical occurrence itself. Vocal method, freed of all but an ideal of the tone to be produced, becomes spontaneous and natural, the tone becomes lovely and free, and the singing becomes sensitive and genuinely musical. Instruction in facts of notation, rhythm, or any other features of the course, then becomes effective, because it is promptly interpreted in terms of interesting musical effect. When, instead of such conditions, the pupils sing noisily and carelessly, when errors are frequent and repeated and arouse no concern, and when all comment and instruction falls on deaf ears, the teacher will do well to lower her voice and see whether she can get music to speak and to be heard. At the beginning its tones will have to be physically present to the ears; but little by little it may be made to enter the restless minds, and from there speak healingly, or it may be with compelling vitality, to the spirits of the children.

CHAPTER TEN

Things and Their Symbols

Things in themselves are interesting. The cargo on the quay, the sound of music in the air, the story from the lips of the story-teller, are fascinating. But bills of lading, notes on the staff, and pages of words in the reader must be met.

The thought of education has always been turned on the vexing problem of making symbols, with which it deals so largely, familiar and unrepellant. We must have symbols. Only by them can we establish means of communication, put our thought into packages, and carry on commerce in material things and in things of the mind and spirit. For things in themselves are localized, they will not traverse space and time. That task their messengers, the symbols, can accomplish. Yet when the life-long labor of becoming familiar with symbols begins, there is danger that things will become lost behind the symbols that should reveal them, and that the fascination they exert will fade and be replaced by indifference or distaste. The child will still run to where the band is playing; but he will turn away from the music lesson when the notes upon the staff confront him.

Arbitrary character of symbols

It is difficult for one who is versed in any group of symbols to realize how utterly destitute of sense or meaning they are to the one who first approaches them. Perhaps teachers, being adepts in that which they teach, are less able than others to recapture the state of mind of the novitiate. The impression of meaningless babble made upon us by conversation in a tongue we do not know, the blank unintelligibility of the figures upon the tea-chest or the Chinese laundryman's slip, should forewarn us. Yet those of us who teach music find it difficult to believe that *do, mi, so,* are wholly toneless to the neophyte, or that a staff with notes upon it may appear to the beginner, as the late lamented Henry Turner Bailey said it was in fact, as a barbed wire entanglement rather than as an invitation to song.

Nor can we easily rid ourselves of the notion that there is something especially appropriate and natural about these symbols, as expressing the meanings they do express, when compared with others. That a swastika sign might, in the beginning, just as well have signified 'flat', or the dollar mark or any other figure have signified 'sharp'—and *meant* it—is almost inconceivable. At five years of age, however, we would have accepted the swastika sign without question. As a more engaging figure, we would probably have preferred it had we been given choice.

How symbols acquire meaning

Our great educator, John Dewey,[1] has told us in clearest language how symbols acquire content and meaning. It is by use. The only way by which *do, mi, so,* acquire tone is by hearing them given tone. Were they sung from the first and always to three consecutive tones of the chromatic scale they would become inseparably attached to those pitches. Having been sung to the tones of the tonic, mediant, and dominant, they are attached, instead, to those. The effort which most persons who read this book will have in applying *do, mi, so,* to a chromatic succession (which they should try to do) may suggest how totally dependent we are upon long continued use for the meanings which symbols hold for us. (The difficulty the skilled adult has in this case is, of course, infinitely greater than that experienced by the child in attaching the usual tones to *do, mi, so;* for the adult has violently to suppress an old established association, while the child has nothing to overcome. Nevertheless, even after the difficulty for the child is thus discounted, the illustration may rightly carry to our imagination some idea of childish perplexities that are often too lightly weighed.)

When meanings are to be attached to symbols, through use, it is important that the usage be unvaryingly correct. The symbols we are discussing now are the *so-fa* syllables. These are nouns, just as cat, dog, rat, mouse, mole, rabbit,

[1] *How We Think:* John Dewey.

squirrel, are nouns. Or perhaps we should say they are nouns, as father mother, brother, sister, aunt, uncle, cousin, are nouns; for that which is named is a relationship not a positive designation. But if, to revert to the first series, the seven little animals were released in the nursery, there to become the subject of a lesson in names, it is evident that some care would have to be exercised lest the child should find himself possessed of seven names and seven animals, but without power to attach the correct name to the right animal. Should the names thus be learned, as a series and by an act of memory, but remain unattached, the child would have acquired more of that fruitless and academic knowledge that the schools, against their best efforts, often impart. Or the child might be told once the correct name for each animal, and then be charged with the responsibility of affixing the names correctly ever after. The result of this would be woful misapplication of names, with the possibility that some names would become forever wrongly attached. The teacher would be in a similar difficulty were seven objects placed before her, and the seven nouns of the Turkish language that named them were then applied. If the seven objects and names ran always in a fixed order, as *do, re, mi, fa, so, la, ti,* (imagining these to be Turkish nouns) the teacher could learn the rigmarole in a few trials. But the teacher herself would realize, with some foreboding, that she might some day meet some of the objects detached from the series, or might meet all of them differently arranged, in any one of countless new orders;

and she would hardly feel that meaning had become reliably attached to any one of the names when only its position in a series protected it. She might reflect that seven new children, John, Mary, Susan, James, William, David and Lucy, would hardly be known to her could she identify them only by their order in a row of seats. Only when each name had become inextricably associated with an individual child, at any time and under any conditions, so that it seemed to have become part of him, would the noun have acquired that strength and richness of meaning that alone would give it value.

Tonal meaning for so-fa syllable-names

While *do* and *re*—if we ignore historical origins and adaptability to vocalization—might as well in the beginning have been *umph* and *humph,* it is possible soon to attach the appropriate tonal meanings to the accepted names with such firmness that they will appear to have resided there by divine right from the beginning of the world. To paraphrase Kipling, in his *Just So* stories, *Do* must have been named *Do* because it sounded like *do;* and since it sounded like *do,* what else was there to name it? Such a result, however, is not to be reached hastily by any driving drill. "Sky" and "tree," or even "automobile" and "telephone," have acquired their connotations, rich, full, and unmistakable, not by any memory drill, but solely by dint of familiar and oft-repeated use. So will the child learn *do* and *re,* as tonal verities, by long and familiar use, and not by zealous instruction.

And this use must be by *imitation.* If too soon the child is asked "how *do* sounds" it is possible that it will not sound at all, or will sound wrongly. Or if asked to sing *do, re,* before the tonal meanings of these have become attached, he may sound *do, mi,* but *call* them *do, re;* and this is equivalent to saying "red, *blue"* when the colors that are to be named are red, *green.* Easy, continued repetition, by means of imitation, over a long series of days, will bring firm possession of the tonal concepts; and no effort to "remember" or ratiocinate his way to the desired conclusion will be half so safe and natural to the child. And if ratiocination is abandoned the scale-pattern will not be adopted as the basis for developing these tone-syllable meanings. Instead, songs will be sung by syllables, by imitation, with the result that musical experience will be richer, and that each tone-syllable will be encountered in innumerable contexts; and it will thereby, in the end, be known by its own quality, and not by its placement in an artificial series.

The *so-fa* syllables, as nouns which become filled with meaning, thus do what all other nouns do; that is to say, they delimit, or set out in sharp definition, a concept that would otherwise be vague. The old metaphysical query as whether there can be thought without language occurs to mind here. We have no reason to discuss it. We may conjecture, however, that should even a dog learn to give one bark for meat and two for water, those two objects would be more sharply differentiated or conceived in his mind than they would be were there no such explicit, differentiated responses.

We have spoken of the *so-fa* syllables and their meanings as they are used in the *Movable Do* system. That which they name might appear to be somewhat indefinite because it is merely a functional quality. But in fact there is no such indefiniteness. Tonic, a point of repose, is no more an elusive concept because the quality is given now to one pitch and now to another, than is 'home' an elusive concept because the family sometime moves into a different house. And all other tones are defined with equal definiteness, because of their proximity or relationship to the tonic, just as all other homes are defined because they are neighboring homes, or because, though perhaps distant, they shelter blood-relatives. In fact these tonal relationships, and not the factor of absolute pitch, constitute the whole order we call music, and are the essence of its structure, quality and meaning. Any names that name relationships as do the harmonic names *tonic, dominant, sub-dominant,* or as do the melodic *Tonic so-fa* syllables, are therefore useful in definitizing essential musical concepts. Absolute pitch, comparatively, is little but a concern of the physicist.

Visual symbols

Teachers of music in public schools appear in general to be quite successful in developing in children accurate and fixed tonal meanings for *so-fa* syllables. It is doubtful, however, whether they are equally successful in training children to attach tonal meanings to the degrees of the staff. The suggestion is made here that the failure, if and when there is failure, may be in some measure due to what can hardly be reckoned as other than a pedagogical error. An investigation of the processes used may at least be worth while.

It was said that meaning or content is acquired through use, and that use must be guarded against error by employing imitation. In connection with the syllables this employment of imitation in some degree is inescapable, since there is no conceivable process by which the child can find for himself the tonal content of *do* or *re,* or can discover, (if we think of his mind moving in the reverse direction) what syllable names should be applied to any tones of the scale that he has previously heard. The syllables applied to the tones of the scale are accordingly very commonly practised by rote, and usually throughout a protracted period, with the result that the association of names and tones becomes firmly established.

But lines and spaces of the staff, at the beginning of the child's dealings with them, are no more eloquent of tone or of tonal relationships than were the *so-fa* syllables. Nevertheless, many teachers who are quite clear as to the value of imitation in connection with the syllables, begin to distrust it when the staff is reached. Assuming that the pupil now knows the scale series, they require him to reckon his way from note to note. If this is to be done

with any degree of facility the pupil must be provided with
note-patterns that employ only conjunct motion; and since
songs in conjunct motion are almost impossible to find,
that requirement further entails the use of artificial exercises. Often, moreover, the preceding rote practice has been
restricted not only to tones in conjunct motion, but either
to the scale as a whole, up and down, or fundamental parts
of it. That is to say, free and varied movement, fluctuating
in its undulations after the manner of a song-melody, even
were that melody in conjunct motion, is likely to be unknown. The technique the pupils have with syllables is
consequently not adapted to the varied, flexible movement
encountered upon the staff; unless, as was said, that movement be so greatly restricted that it consists of little more
than scale passages of the kind previously practised by rote.
But even if these have been provided they must soon be
abandoned, and free movement that employs skips must be
undertaken. In view of that day, which at best can be
postponed only a brief time, and even then to considerable
disadvantage, it is better to conduct the preceding rote practice with syllables on free melodies that contain skips. But
still, in that case the conditions necessary for making the
staff degrees vivid with tonal meaning have not been met;
for the pupil does not know immediately what syllables are
properly attached to the notes he sees, and only those
syllable names can awaken the right tonal associations in
his mind. The process is therefore quite slow and indirect.
The pupil reckons along the scale track until he finds the

syllable names of the notes, and the syllable names then bring the associated memories of tone. But this means that the syllable, rather than the staff itself, holds tonal meanings. The staff, it is hoped, will acquire them by derivation.

Or it should. In practice, however, the set of mind the child employs as he reckons staff-degrees appears to silence effectually his tonal imagination. Always the tense mental effort of computation is accompanied by a peculiar tonelessness and tightness of voice that testifies clearly to this absence of musical ideation. Such ill-success is hardly justified by the argument that it is inescapable, is inseparable from first attempts in all technical study, and will be overcome in good time. This argument fails because the objection is not that the effort is rudimentary in degree, but that it is wrong *in kind*. The purpose of the teaching is to develop musicalness; but this type of effort from the child is either tangential to or subversive of musicalness. Even slower progress and slighter results would be acceptable were the mental movement only in the right direction.

If the child should not reckon upon the staff, or not reckon unduly, then the tonal meanings symbolized by the staff must be gathered through imitation. Most persons will agree, however, that a pure rote process here would not in the end produce skillful reading, however long it were continued. That is to say, mere looking at the notes while their pitches are provided by means of some instrument or by another voice will develop no power. It is essential that the notes be viewed as in some tonal system that has a begin-

ning and end, a top and a bottom, in order that each of
the tones symbolized by a staff-degree may acquire a clear
identity. But this means that each pitch, as symbolized by
a degree called into utterance by a note upon it, shall be
conceived after the manner usually represented by the use
of a noun. It may be, indeed, as some teachers believe, that
the desired tonal concepts could be formed and could become clear (although somewhat awkward to talk about!)
without the use of any names. The concept that is 'tonic,'
'do,' 'one,' 'key-note,' may indeed have some sort of existence in persons who lack any term whatsoever that would
express it. It does seem evident, however, that such awareness would represent only a condition due to impressionability, and not a state of knowing. Aesthetically it may be
significant, but cognitively it is sterile. In brief, it is not a
concept: and some concept there must be, if we are to move
beyond the stage of supine impressionability, even if that
concept be provided with no word by which it can make
itself articulate.

Developing meaning for visual symbols

While names and words may come to overrun thought,
as we shall see in the next chapter, it appears nevertheless
true that notwithstanding the dangers they expose us to
they are indispensable. For the present, then, let us assume
that they are so. At least let us assume that there are concepts that *might* have names attached, whether they do or
should have them or not; and let us assume further, since

we can not without great difficulty describe at length the nature of these concepts, that the *so-fa* syllables may come to define them as well as any other nouns that might have been invented. So established we may then approach our present problem, which is how to attach firmly the meanings that are connoted by the *so-fa* syllables *directly* to the staff.

The answer has been forecast, if not explicitly stated. It is by *singing from the staff by imitation, employing the so-fa syllables.* In the Key of G-major it is quite as important that the second, third and fourth lines of the staff become eloquent of certain tonal meanings as that *do-mi-so* awaken these meanings. And a subtle distinction is here important: *the meaning of the three lines is not first an abstract and toneless do-mi-so that is then to be translated into tone, but the lines and the syllables must be equally authentic symbols of one and the same tonal fact.* That is to say, they are coordinate, and *neither has priority.* The instrumentalist illustrates this clearly. With him the lines and spaces grow eloquent of tone directly, and names such as the vocalist needs are likely to be used only in later designation of tonal concepts that were already explicit as represented by the staff, but that need to be broadened and enriched in the direction implied by the names themselves. The vocalist (as musician), lacking the physiological and mechanical aids by which explicit staff-meanings are so quickly developed for the instrumentalist, must begin with these broader and richer concepts (of tonal relation) by use of the names that connote them, and see that they are attached directly to the staff.

The method by which the vocal musician, in childhood, does this has been stated in general terms, but one observation remains. If rote-practice with syllables, but in entire disconnection with the staff, is too long continued, there is danger that the staff will never gather intrinsic tonal meaning. To give it parity with syllables as a tone-connoting agency, the rote-practice with syllables earlier recommended should, *from the first,* be in connection with the staff-representation of the tones sung. If, for instance, a song— presumably one among many—has been sung by rote by syllables long before the staff is introduced, and if that song, so known, is subsequently placed on the staff before the children as a means of introducing the pitch-symbolization function of the staff, that pitch-symbolization becomes comparatively a superfluous and unessential form of symbolization. To be more explicit, let us suppose that this first staff-pictured song is in the Key of G-major and that its first four tones are *do, re, mi, so.* After continued instruction and repeated singings while looking at the staff, the children will still not observe anything wrong if the teacher surreptitiously changes the position of one of these notes, or, for that matter, the position of several scattered through the song, but will continue in cheerful innocence to sing the notes that *should* be there. If, on the other hand, their first sight of the staff and their first hearing of syllable-names are coincident, staff-position is as eloquent and primary a form of symbolization as are the names themselves.

The suggestion to withhold syllable-names entirely until the staff is introduced, and then to teach them by rote *only in conjunction with the notes on the staff,* may appear doubtful, for it is far from being a common practice. Examination of our methods in instrumental music will reveal, however, that the plan, in its general pedagogical aspect, is not unknown. As a method of teaching children piano, for instance, few teachers would recommend a protracted period in rote-playing, coupled with entire silence about the staff, to be followed by the introduction of the staff, presented first as an agency for representing tunes already known. Instead, every effort is usually made from the first to ensure an association of key (on the keyboard), note (on the staff), and sound (as heard and conceived in association), in which the three factors will be equal and indissoluble. Nothing more is recommended in the field of vocal music.

Instruction in the symbols used to denote rhythm, such as notes, rests, bars, and others, might well have been discussed in this chapter, but the discussion would have been largely repetitive. That is to say, these symbols, like those of pitch, acquire content by use, and this use should *first be inculcated by imitation in connection with the symbols themselves upon the staff, and preferably as employed in a piece of music.* As with pitch-symbols, too, it is important that imitation, or exemplification of forms, be renewed or

continued to such an extent that the learner will be protected against making incorrect responses with the result
that vague, uncertain, or positively wrong connotations will
thereafter be attached to symbols that should hold forever
only exact and unchanging meanings. Perhaps this pedagogical principle is more often disregarded in connection
with rhythmic symbols than it is in connection with pitch,
because the illusion persists that a mathematical knowledge
that can be gained by thought is equivalent to a musical
mastery that can only be gained by practice. The comparatively poor results obtained in most schools in rhythmic
practice may be accounted for in part, perhaps, by precisely
this error.

CHAPTER ELEVEN

Reading Music, and Learning for Reading

Interpreting symbols and reading music

Reading music is something more than interpreting correctly one symbol after another; but the nature of that "something more" is not easily discovered and described. One obvious fact may guide us: and that is that *a single note is not the sign of a musical idea,* as a single word is the sign of an idea, but that a group of notes, as used in forming a motive or a phrase, is rather the sign. Reading of music must therefore concern itself with reading notes connected in a series.

If interpretation of symbols, considered separately as objects awakening conditioned responses, were the equivalent of reading music, one could begin in the middle of a page and then read forward or back with equal facility. Or if the measures were aligned in vertical columns, as well as in horizontal succession, one could move from the second measure in one line to the second measure in the next, and so down the page with a facility equal to that which he would display in moving from measure to measure along one horizontal line. But in neither of the two cases would such equal facility be found; and the reason for failure would be the lack of meaning apparent, not in the symbols themselves, considered separately, but in the musical (or unmusical) succession that would be found so joining them. Musical meaning is thus something apart from the meanings of the symbols separately. In a sense it is not even compounded of them, although collectively they convey it. It is an integrated thought, a unitary movement, which is intelligible in its true meaning only when it is whole. To read music one must seize this meaning. To spell notes and call the act "reading music" is to be guilty of considerable laxity of thought and expression.

A citation from Bergson will afford a mental background upon which we may more readily sketch the particular pattern of thought we would present. Bergson [1] calls attention to the fact that one may follow the poet's verses as a unitary expression, may "enter into his thought," put one's self "into his feelings, live over again the simple state he has broken into phrases and words." And he continues: "I sympathize then with his inspiration, I follow it with a continuous movement which is, like the inspiration itself, an undivided act. Now, I need only relax my attention, let go the tension that there is in me, for the sounds, hitherto swallowed up in the sense, to appear to me distinctly, one by one, in their materiality. For this I have not to do anything; it is enough to withdraw something. . . . Let me go farther still in the direction of dream: the letters themselves will become loose and will be seen to dance along, hand in hand, on some fantastic sheet of paper."

[1] *Creative Evolution:* Henri Bergson.

Precisely similar is the case with a musical composition, however simple. It sang in the mind of the composer as an undivided expression. An act of intuitive penetration will re-create it in the mind of another. *But one condition of such re-creation is a singing state of mind similar to that out of which the composition was born.* 'Relaxation' into dull material sense will reduce the attempted re-creation to a weary and undiscerning recitation of the notes. Lacking the life and insight necessary to participation in the undivided movement, lacking the sense of a goal to which the series tends, the symbols themselves will become comparatively strange and unintelligible. Blundering spelling of notes will then displace reading of music.

Musical experience necessary

The ways, the directions, the goals of musical thought, become discernible, and may be forecast, only in a mind that has become familiar with, and sympathetically intuitive toward, musical thought in general: and such sympathy and understanding can be developed only by the experience of sharing or participating in such thought. The period of rote-singing that precedes all attempts at reading music is consequently a vital phase in the subsequent reading program. The moods of music within which the notes play, the goals sought by phrases and periods, the balances characteristic of melodic undulation, the agreements between part and part with respect to rhythm, all become subconsciously known as a native language, a veritable habit of expression.

But at this point another consideration enters that is often overlooked. If the experience with the language of music is to give a background of understanding from which the pupil will be able to divine the intention that runs through the notes he is to read, then the music that provides the experience, and the music which is subsequently to be read in the light of that experience, should be alike in mood, in length, in musical style, in musical elaborateness or simplicity, and in structure and form. It is difficult to see, for instance, how long experience with elaborate rote songs of a page or two in length, perhaps provided with piano accompaniments that employ harmonies not implied in the melody, and that are so free in expression that they contain few reiterations, sequences or recurrences, can prepare the child to discover the musical meaning that lurks behind the notes in a twelve-measure folk-song built largely of quarter-notes and resting on a clearly-felt basis of tonic and dominant triads: such as, for instance, *Winter, Farewell.* The lack of articulation in such a case may, indeed, produce results that are not only negatively bad but that are positively so. For when reading is attempted in connection with music that voices unfamiliar musical thoughts in an unfamiliar musical style the learner is disconcerted in any effort of musical intuition that he may make, and is driven back upon the necessity of wholly rationalized, note-to-note, spelling.

As a further misfortune, the rote-singing, which gave play to his musical nature, appears as richly interesting and musical, and reading music from the staff as wholly uninteresting and unmusical. A similar misfortune occurs in connection with courses in appreciation, when these give the learner large and elaborate musical experiences, from which he must turn in order to undergo the comparatively juiceless, daily "regular music lesson." There is no need whatever thus to separate the child's musical appetite from the nutritive material upon which the true growth of his musical power depends; and it is a tragic blunder so to separate it.

Notes and the song

The musical experience which makes the soil fecund may be closely articulated with the music study that should follow it, first by restraining unwise ambitions to make the child musically mature in his first year in school, and secondly through aiding his first steps in "reading" by judicious rote-processes. Just as the separate symbols must acquire meaning through practice that employs imitation, so must the thread of meaning that runs through the notes and "swallows" them in a larger movement (to use Bergson's term), be first revealed to the child through a personally conducted tour over the series. A physiological psychology that makes no provision for a continuous act of mind that is other than a succession of discrete "reactions" makes this statement hard to believe. Nevertheless it seems

certain that *meaningful wholes* are discerned by the child
before he discerns *meaningless parts*. This is not to say that
the child sees large things before he sees small ones—
for this could easily be disproven—but it is to say that he
sees the integrated, of whatever size, before he sees the dis-
integrated. In fact, as Will Grant Chambers has said, "education is an oscillation of the mind between ever narrow-
ing limits." This means that "the whole before the parts,"
and a process of analysis, are not meaningless slogans but
are statements of verities. Their meaning, however, has not
always been properly applied. If it had been, we would
understand that notes are not builded into music, but that
music may be broken up into notes. And if the direction
of mental movement so described is followed, we will discover, further, that notes themselves, as separate symbols,
become meaningful only when that meaning becomes functional in contributing to larger meaning. This is merely to
say that a note, as a word, has some meaning in itself, as a
separate symbol, but that its significant meaning is revealed only in connection with its context.

The contextual meanings are revealed—we may even
say that the conception of the possible existence of contextual meaning is revealed—only through experience. The
teacher may teach all the words of the spelling-book or of
the dictionary, but the child will not read except by reading; and that reading—and the very idea of reading—is
caught from hearing reading done. Sooner or later a child
must be introduced by imitation into that continuous sweep

of thought which is comparable to the flight of a bird. The curve of the flight can be broken theoretically into a series of points, each of which becomes fixed and immobile as we consider it; and similarly the sweep of melody can be broken into a series of tones (or of notes) each of which, if we stop to examine it, becomes a halting point and destroys the song.

In much so-called sight-reading this latter unmusical, disjunct, process is rigidly exacted until the last note has been disposed of. But the song, *as* a song, then remains to be learned. To integrate the dismembered fragments is the next problem. It would be amusing, if it were not piteous, to see how the heroic teacher, who has thus far exacted "independent effort," then capitulates. With the voice or piano she assembles the fragments, marshals them into musical order, and leads the children triumphantly through their meaning. The consummation is reached. They have the song. But in the end they have gained it by following a lead or imitating an example that supplied something that was not even dimly forecast in their own minds. The song is learned, in fact, as purely by imitation as it would have been had the pupils been led at the beginning. This is what was meant by our statement that *sooner or later* the integrated product would have to be heard.

The further question now is whether the hearing should be sooner or later: and the answer is, sooner; for when the requisite illumination is wholly withheld until the end, it never quite shines away the dark errors and blind spots left by the halting struggle. The song, that is to say, is never quite the unified and whole creation it should have been; and in general the pupils have not yet discovered, of their own efforts, how notes run together collectively to create music such as they are familiar with when notes are absent.

Two directions for mental effort

The singing of *songs* by syllables by imitation, while the pupils follow the notation, must be far other than a performance by the teacher which the children hear but to which they do not attend or contribute. It must be conceded that all rote and imitative work may thus become a mere hurling of sensations against a heedless sensorium until, in spite of unreceptivity, the resistant walls are penetrated and some marks are graven on the obdurate substance within. Such rote work is, of course, almost worthless; and a desire to spur greater pupil-activity accounts for the practice of withdrawing all aid or example on the part of the teacher in favor of "independent effort." But when, as in attempts to sing at sight, such effort is obviously unprepared and incompetent to reach the proper goal, and when to persist in it may mean failure on the particular song and damage to the child's general musical understanding and interest, the teacher has merely exchanged one kind of failure for another. True, the teacher may yet prefer the second one: for failure in being sufficiently musical and skillful as a teacher to hold the interest of the

children to music is likely to appear as a fault in the
teacher; while failure of a class to sing a song at sight
appears to be, whether it is or not, a fault in the children,
for which the teacher may not be blamed, but for which
the children may be chided.

That one learns only when one's own mind acts is
obvious enough. It does not follow, however, that action is
impossible on material that is given the mind whole—as a
line of notes taught by rote—but is guaranteed if a con-
cealed end is sought by a laborious ratiocinative process.
Both modes of engaging the mind are needed. They are
not, however, equally appropriate at different times, in
connection with different subjects; and they are not equally
appropriate with all ages of pupil, even when subject and
problem remain unchanged. Religion, the arts, manners,
and morals, probably need example and revelation more
than do natural sciences and mathematics. In music, in
particular, and with respect to reading printed music, an
intelligent adult, with a rich understanding of music but
who has yet never learned to read it, may well attack the
study in a wholly rational frame of mind. His musical
understanding will not be jeopardized, his long experience
with printed books will aid him, and his adult mind will
lend itself readily to such an approach. In the case of a
child of seven to nine years of age this same important condition will not, however, exist. Strong motivation toward
reading music can not be assumed, musicianly ideals and
understandings have not yet been developed, interest in

music itself will need to be safeguarded, and the rational mode of solving problems—which at best hardly helps him musically—is not yet his mode. Teaching very generally recognizes many of these conditions in his case by giving him a large amount of rote-singing. Our thought now is that the rote-process is not always extended in the right directions, nor made to fulfill certain functions which it alone can fulfill well.

Learning as imprinting

Meumann [1] discusses learning very largely from the standpoint of imprinting. From the point of view maintained here, the study of staff-notation by young children can best be discussed in similar terms. Mastery of oral and visual symbols, the sympathetic understanding of the language of music itself, depend to an unusual degree upon a mental content impressed by experience rather than obtained by reasoning. Learning music is, in short, largely dependent upon first-hand experience graven on memory.

If this be true, the rightness and vividness of the experience are of first importance. To ratiocinate one's way to a conclusion—as, for instance, the time-values of notes in Dvorak's *Humoresque*—may appear to require more effort at learning, but if the notes and music could be seen and heard in memory in association, even while the mathematical terms were very vague in the mind, the learning would be more authentic. From this standpoint we may

[1] *The Psychology of Learning:* Ernst Meumann.

say, indeed, that the strength of learning (or of teaching) is not defined in terms of the laboriousness or independence of the effort at learning that is put forth, but is defined in terms of the accuracy, vividness, and permanency of the imprint. The creaking of the mental machinery, so to speak, is thus not a reliable sign of the rightness or completeness of the learning.

Now all imprints in music attain greatest accuracy, vividness, and permanency when they are connected with the musical impression itself. The symbols, indeed, are meaningless without this; but even the words of songs gather meaning and find permanent place in memory—even the memories of persons not particularly musical—when thus borne "on the wings of music."

The imitative practice herein advocated in connection with sight-singing therefore presents that which we wish learned in a form most favorable for learning. The teacher shows or tells "how it goes." If the pupils remember and respond rightly, and if again to-morrow they remember and respond rightly, the teacher has taught and the pupils have learned. Telling *is* teaching, it would seem, when the pupils thus learn what has been told.

Mental effort in imitative learning

But, as stated earlier, blind and automatic repetition would not represent learning. The response must be consciously and intelligently imitative. The assumption often made with respect to imitation, that it is destitute of any contribution from the imitator's mind, is quite unfounded. At its lowest, as in the elementary stages of learning by rote, it may be thus mechanical. But the very word *imitation* connotes conscious observance of the features that are imitated; and the use of the *example,* which presupposes a high degree of alert intelligence that makes judgments and independent adaptations, is accepted as valid at any stage of work in all kinds of teaching and learning.

Learning by *rote* should thus pass to learning by *imitation* and thence to learning from *exemplification.* This mode of learning can never be wholly abandoned, and an attempt to abandon it in any phase of teaching music would be injudicious. No verbal explanation of *mordent* or *turn,* no description of phrasing or of style, no analysis of 5/4 rhythm, no calculation of the rhythm of the dotted eighth-note followed by the sixteenth-note, is so illuminating as an illustration. And in the rudimentary stages of singing at sight, although the notation is very simple, no directions or descriptions will take the place of imitative or aided response, that may range from almost the stage of mechanical rote to the final stage of occasional illuminating brief exemplification.

Analysis of experience

The weakness of teaching by such a method is not inherent in the method itself, but is due to imperfect uses of the method. The teacher, having led with the model, may conclude she has taught. She has: but have the pupils

learned? Collectively they may have given satisfactory response; but how much of this was mechanical imitation
and how many individuals trailed along in mechanical
imitation of the others? At this stage, even if pupils have
been alert, teaching has only begun. For learning is not
only experience, and memory of that experience, it is also
analysis of that experience. The method here advocated
assumes that the experience, protected against distortion
and failure, should come first, rather than be an end-result
of analysis. But this does not imply that analytical knowledge and the power it carries with it are renounced.

If the pupils, following the printed notation, and using
the *so-fa* syllables, have sung a song entirely by imitation
—for if they follow the notation it is hardly rote-singing—
the teacher has taught not only the tune, movement, and
musical quality of the song. In addition she has taught the
syllable-names of the tones in it, the syllable-names borne by
the staff-degrees in the given key, and the time-values of
the notes. At any rate, subconscious knowledge of these is
now in the minds of the pupils. That knowledge must now
be made conscious and be put in the mind of every individual. By individual singing on alternate phrases; by
syllabification of fragments hummed by the teacher (with
books closed or the notation removed from sight); by
blackboard writing, or by individual writing on music
paper, of such fragments; by these and other processes the
values inherent in the lesson may be capitalized. Such efforts
at confirming and making clear and explicit the knowledge

gained are superior to earlier analytic study because the notes are now eloquent with tonal and musical meanings. The student of harmony who would analyze and write out the chord-scheme of a composition that was freshly ringing in his mind, as compared with stringing chords together toward an unconceived goal, would have much the same musical and educational experience that the child would have in the case described.

From the specific to the general

Probably it is clear that succeeding songs in the same key, and after that succeeding songs in other keys, will need to depend less and less upon imitation. In the upper grades imitation disappears almost completely, and only exemplification of new tonal or rhythmic features is needed. Perhaps an exception must be made when compositions in an entirely new style are undertaken. There, although the old familiar notes remain, they do not carry the same musical meanings. High school pupils suddenly turned into modal music of strange rhythm, or a player wholly trained in classical piano music suddenly confronted with manuscript jazz in a vaudeville orchestra pit, would find themselves singularly unprepared. This is additional evidence, if any is needed, that reading music is not wholly a rational process of translating symbols, and that it therefore needs musical experience, with resultant intuition and anticipation of musical drifts, to make it effective.

Words and symbols as displacing concepts

Before leaving an over-long chapter a word more may be said about the use or non-use of the *Movable Do* syllables as an aid to sight-singing. In the preceding chapter we considered these syllables as names for tonal effects. We must now consider them as names for staff-degrees that temporarily represent those tonal effects. Many teachers have found the efforts of children to puzzle out these names so tyrannous a process and seemingly so subversive of geniune musicalness, that they have sought to dispense with them entirely. And all teachers have encountered disadvantages and dangers in their use to such an extent that they are likely to regard efforts to abandon them with lively interest and sympathy.

The problem is complicated, probably, by the non-use of imitation in teaching these syllables in application to staff-degrees. *Do* consequently becomes a mere *name,* and the location of *this name* is to be found upon the staff. But while reckoning upon the staff to locate this name (as well as all the other names), the tonal reality that is so named drops out of the mind of the pupil. The noun, in short, becomes a symbol of a place instead of a sound. Were the place equally a symbol of sound, this abstraction would not occur.

The danger that a word, which is the sign of an idea, may thus come to be an idea in itself, and so supplant the thing it was intended to intensify, is ever present in the use of all words and symbols. Words may take the place of thought as well as express it. All teaching has to be on guard against the tendency of pupils to handle symbols dextrously rather than they conceive vividly the realities beneath. In the case of the *so-fa* syllables, it appears that the tonal meanings of these symbols are weakened when the staff is studied, while, at the same time, the staff-symbol does not acquire the power of tonal representation that it should have. But it is highly questionable, on the other hand, whether the staff-degrees will acquire more of that power if we do not name them anything. There will, it is true, come forth from the pupil, if we do not name them anything, an ardent effort to conceive the tones that is in itself a highly educational activity. That is to say, if no names stand between the thing in itself and the concept, the child can sing nothing at all until he has, or thinks he has, the concept; and he seeks for it with prayerful intensity. Give him a name, on the other hand, and he can readily sing or utter the name, while only a dim concept, or a wrong concept, or none at all, exists in his consciousness.

But because words can thus take the place of thought, it is not proven that thought would, on the whole, move forward more securely or quickly without words. Words indeed, may be so used as to win triumphantly the concept that would otherwise be sought so earnestly but gropingly in their absence. That we do not fill the syllables, or that we do not fill the staff-symbol, with this rich and triumphant meaning, is not due to any fault inherent in words or symbols, but is rather due to some ill-success in our use of them. In brief, our trouble with *so-fa* syllables, and with all of our symbols, appears to lie in our imperfect use of them. And the remedy for poor use, or abuse, of symbols, is probably to be sought, not in disuse, but in better use.

SPECIFIC FORMS OF PRACTICE

CHAPTER TWELVE

Playing and Singing: Processes and Reactions

The development of instrumental music in the schools of the United States, as seen in the growth of orchestras, bands, violin classes, piano classes, classes in heterogeneous instruments, has been nothing short of phenomenal. No comparable movement in education in music has ever been witnessed in any other country; and it is safe to say that chiefly by means of it was our public school music able to escape from a prolonged childhood and struggle toward citizenship in the world of music as that world is known to musicians. For such an achievement, and despite the fact that all activities in public school instrumental music have not been of an exalted kind, it is entitled to lasting gratitude and honor.

Why instrumental music led the way

For several reasons instrumental music was well fitted to take thus the part of emancipator. In a sense it is the music of musicians. That is to say, it depends upon the development of a specialized musical technique that only those of special musical interests and capacities are likely to have acquired in any considerable degree. The grade teacher, upon whose burdened shoulders the greater part of the teaching of music at first rested, could consequently acquit herself creditably only so long as the course was limited to the teaching of small songs and the rudiments of staff-notation. Again, instrumental music is more specifically musical than song because its entire appeal lies in the musical field and is not derived from associated interests connoted by a song text. For this very reason, however, the grade teacher was again at ease in vocal music, since she could find interest and meaning in songs when she might have been comparatively at a loss to find them in instrumental pieces. But as specially trained musicians entered the public schools in larger numbers, and as music gradually gained in the curriculum, largely as a result of their efforts, a place in which they could extend their teachings, it was inevitable that they should explore in children the interest in sheer tonal art that had earlier captivated them and absorbed so much of their thought. When they did this, the astounding response of pupils and public alike bore witness to the depth and breadth of the genuine musical interests that had slumbered unguessed below the level of the elementary school music program. Perhaps the response, indeed, gave evidence, also, of a combination of manual and musical predilections that were distinctively American; for the continued accomplishments of America in the professional orchestral field are surely significant of more than a passing caprice. However that may be, the response was great enough to cause a reaction in favor of still more musicianly training for public school music teachers; and these, in turn, brought forth still more stimulating responses. Thus, through action and interaction, the impressive achievements now observable throughout the land were finally reached.

Instrumental music not a universal medium

But while instrumental music opened the gates to a wider and more mature field of music, it can not by itself lead to a consummation of all that may be desired in the way of musical education for the masses. One of its shortcomings is that it can not approach universality as nearly as can vocal music. Not only does it require special equipment, not given at birth or in infancy, but compared with vocal music it demands, for the attainment of comparable musical results, a much greater amount of time and effort in specialized study. In short, the distinctive musicianly character that gives it leadership, at the same time denies to it the capacity for universal application. If it were pursued to the point requisite for musicianly performance, it would require an amount of time that could be granted only to the few who wish to specialize; and if all pursued it on the ordinary time-allotment, the results would be too rudimentary to enable it to fulfill its mission.

Another difficulty in the way of a program of instrumental music for all is the nature of the musical instruments that must be used. Many of these—indeed, most of them—are not practicable for children in the lower grades of the elementary school, and a few are usable only by pupils of at least junior high school age. During these same years the vocal music possible to these pupils, though perhaps of simpler texture, may be marked by great musical refinements. In the light of the arguments in an earlier chapter,[1] this point is important; for, if these arguments are accepted, the fact that the vocal material appropriate to the young pupils might be comparatively simple and childlike is of no consequence, the paramount consideration at this point being the attainment of beautiful musical effect rather than the rehearsing of elaborate compositions.

Instrumental music for leisure time

A further limitation of instrumental music as a possible pursuit for all pupils, and as we view it in bands and orchestras of the types now maintained in many schools, is found when we consider it as providing for leisure-time activities. Many of the instruments, it is true, are ideally fitted to provide for cultural enjoyment; but it is equally evident that many of them can have little outcome in the cultural preoccupations of adult life except under a sort of organization that reflects vocational and professional, or at least social outcomes, rather than amateur musical propensities. It is difficult to see, for instance, how a tuba in the hands of a youth, or a bass viol in the hands of a high school girl, is to minister to the cultural life of the player

[1] Chapter VIII: *Musical Responses in Relation to Musical Materials.*

in the days to come. For culture is a fragile flower of the spirit, whatever those who educate for "society" may say; and it requires for its nurture some sheltering from the brisk winds that blow ever through the open doors of gregarious living. It is not without significance to this thought that Santayana [1] makes a distinction between the happiness that comes from satisfactory adjustments and that which comes from the love of beauty, and decides that "social and gregarious impulses, in the satisfaction of which happiness mainly resides, are those in which beauty finds least support." Some measure of freedom of the soul, gained at a distance from the more regimented activities that characterize the social pursuit of music, is necessary to that play of feeling and imagination in which individuality and personal culture come to richest maturity. The large organization may utilize and reflect individual powers, but should not be expected to create them. And unless provision is made for this individual communing with the subject, the final aim of art will be but imperfectly attained.

The small instrumental ensembles that are now being fostered in our schools extend immeasurably the power of instrumental music to contribute to the life we vision as appropriate to the new leisure. The music they use can not dazzle with the pomp and brilliancy that invest the music for symphonic orchestras and bands. Less pretentious than those, it domiciles itself nearer the hearthstone. Since the component instruments of any such group are few, each

[1] George Santayana: *The Sense of Beauty.*

must seek to be, however simple the composition, an effective, expressive, solo voice. Music that can be reflected upon, and each part of which has significance when it is alone, is the result. And in the small ensemble, the large objective stir attendant upon setting an orchestra into action, and which tends to overpower the voices of music that would speak in the mind, is greatly reduced. Even instruments that ordinarily find place only in symphonic organizations therefore disclose unsuspected possibilities when employed in the small group. And as a literature for every sort of small combination is now being developed with uncommon zeal and discernment, the outlook for this phase of instrumental music is very bright.

The need for evaluation of instrumental and vocal music

But instrumental music, at first developing brilliantly, and later searching for a home on less effulgent stages, still can not reach everyone. It is desirable, indeed, that equally with vocal music it should endeavor to do so, because it contributes to musical understanding and enjoyment something that vocal music can not contribute in equal measure. It is equally true, though, that vocal music, in its turn, can contribute much that instrumental music can not contribute in equal measure. It would be a mistake, further, to suppose that the one contribution is greater or more precious than the other. Accordingly it is to the peculiar values of each that we next direct our inquiry. It is timely to do so because, as this is written, the continued growth of bands, orchestras, and classes in instrumental technique has been checked by the economic depression, which has made the purchase of instruments difficult at the same time that it has clouded the outlook for their future vocational use. And meanwhile a movement in vocal music has begun, so rich in promise that a development in it is forecast that bids fair to parallel that which has taken place in instrumental music. If, therefore, we can make now a careful evaluation of the two fields, we may be in better position to conserve and balance the values in both, at a time when transition and uncertainty beset us.

Contrasts

The breach between singers and players of musical instruments is one of such long standing that it may be said to have become traditional. Ordinarily the players of instruments appear to have the better of it. They assume, and with considerable justice, that as a class they have greater technical knowledge of music, and an understanding of it that is specifically musical rather than dramatically emotional. They are confirmed in this opinion because, in their accompanying of singers, they observe that the latter are somewhat uncertain of niceties of intonation, rhythm, and tone-quality, that to an instrumentalist of equal rank are primary considerations. Such disregard of essential elements of tonal discourse in favor of a type of expression that seeks other than formal musical values, appears to the instrumentalist an act of musical apostasy.

Had singers recognized more generally the musical basis of song, as do the best of the *lieder* singers, a large amount of misunderstanding might have been avoided. To the extent that melody, as an absolute musical structure, is given consideration, to that extent are the singer and the player on common ground. But even should musical factors thus occupy the focus of attention, voice and instrument would not be alike.

The musical worlds of the singer and the player would still differ, although now specifically rather than generically, in the way that the musical worlds of the pianist and the violinist differ. In other words, when the voice is conceived instrumentally, as an instrument for producing absolute musical values, it still will have a style that intrinsically is different from that of any other instrument. At first glance this style would appear to be conditioned solely by the nature of the mechanism; but we must not forget that an artistic nature that corresponds to and is attracted by certain expressive possibilities of the instrumentality, seizes on it and forms its style—or its styles—not more in accordance with the instrumental possibilities themselves than in accordance with artistic desires that ever seek to explore and extend those possibilities. The artist is therefore not enslaved to a machine, but artist and instrument, the subjective core and the objective means, react to one another and become one. But of the two complementary factors, the one that is first and causative, and that must certainly be so considered by the educator (lest he turn mechanic) is the subjective.[1]

Organ and instrument

In vocal art, then, considered as a medium of purely musical expression, as it would be were words unknown, are factors of feeling, ideation and production that distinguish it sharply from the art connected with the playing of any musical instrument whatsoever. In the first place, the voice is hardly an *instrument,* in the sense that we ordinarily attach to the word. That is to say, it is not a manufactured object, detached from our organism, and altogether consciously and objectively manipulated. It is thus an organ, rather than an instrument, or is, in fuller statement, a part of our organism without which we would not be complete; and as such it is more directly and intimately a medium for the expression of whatever may be in us than any artificial instrument can possibly be. It is, in fact, revealing; and its disclosures are so frank and personal, that many a lad, at an age when he is reticent and sensitive, avoids baring himself vocally, although willingly expressive through the interposed medium of a 'cello. This is not to say, however, that the voice is a superior medium for musical expression, but only that it may gravitate toward a different quality of expression—which, indeed, we have

[1] For an excellent argument in support of an idealistic philosophy for educators, the reader is referred to a book, *The Reform in Education,* by Giovanni Gentile, translated by Dino Bigongiari.

seen it do. The implication may be, instead, that as a medium for purely musical expression the voice may be comparatively uncertain and tangential. It is not, as are specific musical instruments, specialized. It is rather a vehicle for the expression of much that is human but not musical, whereas the fabricated instrument is designed to voice nothing but musical ideas. If this be true, vocal music will always have to guard itself against loss of clear vision with respect to its possible musical goal; and at the same time, instrumental music will have to be on guard lest it become artificial and detached, through its comparative separation from the subjective core that seeks voice through it.

Stability in pitch

The difference between organ and instrument is fundamental, and will come to mind more than once as we investigate differences in detail. In the matter of intonation, for instance, very marked differences appear. A musical instrument is primarily a mechanism for producing pitches, and is given a rigidity sufficient to ensure unwavering retention of a given pitch, once that pitch has been produced. In the case of keyboard instruments, no sustained muscular tension whatsoever is essential to maintenance of the given pitch, after its initial moment. The stringed instruments require somewhat more of muscular fixation, it is true, and the wind instruments still more. In the case of the voice, however, pliable, living tissues, unassisted by any mechanism, must become fixed in delicate adjustments so long as the pitch is steadfastly maintained. Because, since opportunities for practice are unlimited, this ability has been commonly attained—whatever much harassed music critics may say!—we are likely to overlook the greatness of such an achievement. It can be estimated rightly only when we reflect that it is a comparatively recent attainment. Savage and barbaric peoples seldom give examples of it. Indeed, in singing the music of these peoples, it is often necessary to discard level intonation, and scoop into pitches and waver around them, in order to secure authentic character. A barbaric song, sung with organ-like precision and maintenance of pitch, would be denatured. Nor do speech and ordinary vocal usages, as revealed by infants and adults, characteristically seek level tone. Yet there must be a more or less distinct concept or ideal of fixed musical tone, otherwise it would not be sought in the construction of primitive instruments, where, as in voice, the tendency toward a definite tonation has constantly been manifest. Possibly, however, the aim would be attained and made conscious earlier in instrumental than in vocal explorations. In that case voice may have borrowed level intonation from its instrumental companion, as, for instance, it probably borrowed the trill. Only, in the case of intonation, there may be fewer than in the case of the trill who will suggest that it is high time to return the borrowed feature to the lender.

The tendency of the voice toward instability in pitch—

a tendency intrinsic in the organ—becomes a virtue in speech, where sensitive inflections in pitch constitute the chief expressive factor. The "tone of voice" in which even a single word may be uttered—as, for instance, "no?" or "no!"—is largely determined by pitch inflections. But in song (if and when the musical ideal is or should be pursued) such pitch fluctuations become, instead, an offense to art. Fortunately, our control of our voices is sufficient to enable us to maintain a level pitch, once we desire it. The substitution of the musical ideal for that of human expression is almost the only requirement.

Intonation

The instability of vocal tone does not account for vocalists singing off pitch with a wavering—or unwavering!—tone. That fault, when displayed by a singer whose pitch-perception is normal, arises from a deflection of attention to other than musical considerations—specifically, to the dramatic emotions connected with the text. If these are thought to be of paramount importance, the ear will of course not exercise its proper functions. Even musical quality of tone, as well as intonation, may be sacrificed to expressional endeavors. That an "emotion of life" has little poignancy of appeal until the sensibilities of the hearer are first captivated by the seemingly irrelevant factor of sheer beauty appears to be a truth that is overlooked. With respect to deviation from key, however, it must be said that, although delinquencies of the kind are not thereby excused, the singer nevertheless lacks some mechanical aids toward the attainment of correct pitch that are always at hand to safeguard the instrumentalist. A pitch, for the latter, is at least located somewhere in space, as on the piano keyboard; or it may be reliably evoked by some overt physiological action that is definitely observable. It does not have to be summoned out of the void by an act of pure ideation, and be produced by muscular processes that leave no definite trace behind. Observations of youthful instrumental players tuning, and of older instrumentalists attempting to sing chromatic passages at sight, tend to lead one to the conclusion that the help which the instrumentalist thus receives from his instrument is no small factor in preserving his reputation for superiority in intonation.

Reading Music

The disparity between singing and playing is nowhere more clearly apparent than in connection with reading music from the staff. Here the advantage in favor of the players of most instruments is stupendous; and the advantage is great even to a player on such an instrument as the French horn. A degree of the staff, indeed, becomes for most instrumentalists equivalent to the location in space of a precise pitch; and it thus acts as a definite symbol that sets off a physical action that brings the proper pitch with a mechanistic certainty as reliable as that of a photo-electric cell. Any instrumental musician worthy of the name does, indeed, conceive the tones represented by the notes before he hears them produced; but it is not absolutely essential to their production that he do so. It is possible for him, in reading new music, to strike a note—as we have all seen pianists do—look at it sharply (under the impression that he has blundered) and come to the conclusion that he was right, after all. But this means that he certainly did not conceive the tone aright before he played it; and thus to produce a tone correctly, after having conceived it wrongly or not at all, would be quite impossible to the vocalist.

If vocalists do not read music at sight as well as instrumentalists—and it must be admitted that they do not—it is because the sheer musical power requisite to their doing so is much greater than that required of the instrumentalist. Only by a powerful grasp of tonality, which is to say by an act of musical imagination that would rest upon a broad knowledge of schemes of musical organization, could a vocalist proceed with entire security along the path of even a diatonic melody. If his part were highly chromatic, as in most modern music, the task would become a superlative test of musicianship. To succeed in it the reader would have to recognize modulations, harmonic and detached intervallic relationships, and, in extreme cases, would need to be endowed with an infallible sense of absolute pitch. Nor could he succeed with this equipment by reading his single melodic line alone. Instead, he would necessarily comprehend the entire tonal organization, and would exercise precisely the kind of effort that the orchestra leader makes when he silently studies, and seeks to hear in imagination, his score. No effort equal in degree, and no effort quite comparable in kind, is required of any instrumentalist.

Rhythm in voice

In speaking of the muscular processes by which the vocalist produced tones of certain pitch, we said that such muscular action left no trace behind. Put in technical terms, this amounts to saying that the kinesthetic response is so slight as to be negligible. This is not more true in connection with pitch adjustments, however, than it is in connection with rhythm; and again here the experience of the instrumentalist is much more helpful than that of the vocalist toward developing substantial technical knowledge and skill.

For rhythm, as we have said, although it may enter by the ear, establishes itself in reality only when extended through the physical organism: and if that organism engages largely in the initial rhythmic experience, rhythm will be conceived—having been lived—with a strength and reality that will not inhere in the concept of it gained when rhythm reverberates only faintly in the organism as an echo from the small aural mechanism alone. The tap dancer, for illustration, must have a far deeper experience of the rhythm he dances than that gained by the person who hears only the rhythmic tatoo of the dancer's feet.

But from this point of view, rhythm as lived is compared only with rhythm as heard; and what we have to investigate is rhythm as lived by the singer in comparison with rhythm as lived by the player of a musical instrument. That difference is one that again exists between organic and efficient action; and at that point we must seek it.

Action that is wholly organic is largely involuntary and subconscious. Most of our organic life goes on below the surface of our attention, and certainly without our volition. Certain organic functions may, indeed, come into our consciousness, and may be controlled. Breathing is an excellent example of such a function. But even when we become conscious of breathing, and exert control over it, it remains largely automatic. Certainly it leaves no very vivid or definite kinesthetic memories. For instance, when breath is directed against the vocal cords, for the production of tone, we feel no detail of its mode of action. Or, again, when it is released by diaphragmatic action, we learn of the control only by vague sensations in the costal muscles. When, however, the tone, though produced by a steady flow, is articulated by the tongue or lips, these being voluntarily controlled, we do acquire a clear sense of the rhythmic divisions. That is to say, in this last case the tongue (in particular) may become subject to voluntary and definite control that in type approaches the control exerted in manipulation. A larger degree of consciousness is then present, and there is considerable kinesthetic memory. Such comparative weakness of rhythmic sense as remains is due to the fluidity, the flexibility of organic action, as a result of which each movement merges into the next rather than is displaced by the next.

Rhythm in playing

Now an instrument, made the object of organic action, adds precisely this mechanical, clock-like division of time and action. Even the action of the tongue in triple-tonguing, as in playing a trumpet solo, becomes an act of mechanical precision to a degree greater than that which characterises the act when the same effect is produced vocally. At first glance little would seem to have been added; but on re-flection we find that lip sensations are added in the case of the trumpeter, and moreover his changes of pitch, to which the triplet tones must be nicely timed, are signalized by definite manipulations of valves, or at least by definite changes in lip-tension, that mark these moments out as larger divisions within which the smaller moments must play with the utmost precision. A rollicking song in six-eighths measure is therefore still something less saliently and exactly rhythmical than even the same melody per-formed on trumpet—not to mention the triple-tongued solo. It must be admitted, in addition, that the focus of attention of both the singer and his hearer, since word-meanings must be attended to, differs from that of the player and his hearer. Moreover, each note of the song, due to demands of the text, changes its vowel-quality; and this change of tone-color deflects attention to some extent, in comparison with an instrumental tone, from both the rhythmic and melodic organization of the music. That is but another aspect of the difference between the instrument, which is formed for purely musical purposes, and the voice, which lends itself, among other functions, to the production of music. But even were the voice to sing all the triplet tones to the same vowel and syllable, as it sometimes does when it essays vocal accompaniments cast in instrumental style, it would still lack something of the rhythmic positiveness of the instrumental production, both to the singer in particular, and in some degree to the hearer. For one difference yet remains; and that is that the "speaking-moment" of a tone alone places it rhythmically. In many instruments this speaking-moment of a tone tends to be the moment when the volume of sound is greatest. The ictus or stroke on the tone becomes thus, in some cases, almost obtrusively salient. But in voice the contrary tendency prevails. At the moment of beginning the vocal tone is always likely to possess smaller power than it acquires a moment later. Only by packing breath against the throat and releasing it—with abominable effect, of course!—explosively, can the vocalist parallel the effect natural to the piano, plucked-string instruments, and most wind-instruments, as these are ordinarily played. Even the bowed strings are more reliably played when at least some slight emphasis of attack is sought. Only the Aeolian harp therefore appears to parallel exactly the manner of attack upon tones that is characteristic of the voice, particularly when a vowel sound is initiated.

Various instruments in relation to rhythmic development

When we turn our attention to the manipulation of instruments the greater reaction in favor of rhythmic development that accrues to the player, as compared with the singer, discloses itself in full. The wind instruments exhibit, perhaps, the smallest degree of superiority, and much has already been said about these. We should add, however, that the fingering of the flute and the other woodwinds necessitates neural promptings and muscular actions that register themselves in kinesthetic memory with far greater authenticity and vividness than do the comparable actions of the singer. In support of that statement we may adduce here the observation that any woodwind player is likely, in silent study or recall of a line of music, to image his performance of it quite clearly in terms of manipulatory movements; and the singer certainly does not have this kinesthetic imagery to an equal extent.

When we pass to the strings of the orchestra, not only are the left-hand sensations stronger, because of the greater strength of action requisite to firm stopping of the strings, but the bowing arm, with attendant play of large muscles, lives the rhythm in an extraordinary manner. Curiously, however, because of the sensitivity of the hand and fingertips, and partly, perhaps, because the bow is likely to reflect the rhythm of the notes less persistently (on account of slurred bowings) than do the fingers, the kinesthetic imagery of rhythmic character that remains is likely to be more largely connected with the fingering than with the bowing.

Finally, in connection with piano, the sharp sensations from the finger-tips reinforce the rhythmic sense almost as would a tatoo beaten upon the skin. With the two hands under the necessity of coordinating diverse rhythms, a further factor toward rhythmic organization and reaction is added. Of all the instruments except those of percussion, its tone is moreover characterized by greatest proportionate initial strength, with the result that every tone it produces thus establishes a rhythmic moment with extraordinary positiveness. This instrument thus tends to establish itself as an exponent of rhythm to a degree greater than any other, unless we except the instruments of the percussion group. Its tendency, indeed, is toward the mechanically rhythmic; and this tendency has to be opposed by those who would express themselves musically through its mediation, just as the tendency to neglect something of formal, rhythmic organization, in styles of music that rightly require it, must be overcome by those who would express themselves through the voice.

CHAPTER THIRTEEN

Singing and Playing: Processes and Values

No positive can fail to imply its negative: what a thing is not is defined when we have stated what it is. In the preceding chapter tendencies toward sins of omission (in terms of what the other might supply) were accordingly found in connection both with instrumental and with vocal music, even while the virtues of each were extolled. Neither was thereby disparaged in any but a faintly negative sense. We merely found that they are different in kind rather than unequal in worth. In our analysis of what each is and is not, however, the positive values of instrumental music formed our point of departure and received the greater emphasis. In the present chapter we will therefore first emphasize more particularly the positive values of vocal music.

Let us first recall the comparative shortcomings that we attributed to vocal music. It was found to be less purely and specifically musical than instrumental music, and therefore to be less attentive to essentials of absolute music, such as tone, pitch, and rhythmic form. It was found, also, to be of such a nature that its practice did not contribute, equally with instrumental music, to the easy development of technical power, with respect to quick and accurate read-

ing from the staff. But these are comparative shortcomings;
and on the other hand, vocal music is saved, by their very
possession, from the danger that often confronts instrumental music, of becoming merely mechanistically competent. We may find, now, that further virtues may be hidden
behind its seeming incompetences.

Tonal concepts, pure and adulterated

One virtue the vocal approach unquestionably possesses,
and that virtue is of such promise and magnitude that many
less fundamental ones may well be relinquished in its stead.
Tone and music, as conceived by the vocalist, may easily
come to be purer, and more idealistic, more detached from
any taint of materiality, than when conceived by any other
musical mind, with the exception only of that of the composer. For the very mechanism that gives the instrumentalist his hold on pitch and rhythm also tends to vitiate the
purity of his tonal concepts. This is because along with his
tonal concept he inevitably carries non-tonal percepts and
kinesthetic memories. The tone he conceives is not wholly
a disembodied voice, made meaningful only by its relationship to other disembodied tones in an idealistically perceived series. It is a conceived tone; but it is also a movement, a location indicated by physical landmarks, and a
sensation in the hand, or in some other part of the anatomy,
even at the moment that it becomes a tone to the ear.

How great such obscuration of the tonal concept may be
is best seen by observing young instrumentalists in be-

ginning stages of their instruction—as, for instance, those in a violin class. Their eyes are bright with an objectively-focused gaze, their muscles are tense with the premonition of immediate and imperative action. It is obvious, as their gaze concentrates upon a note, that they are seeking to translate it into a designated physical response. But how clearly and accurately is the indicated tone resounding meanwhile in their minds? Often, we are bound to answer, it is hardly preconceived at all, but comes forth as an extrinsic and somewhat surprising happening, to which small attention need be paid. Later, of course, the physical movements, as a result of extended practice, become mechanical, and the pupil may come to conceive the tone directly from the staff. But two dangers nevertheless have supervened. One is that the pupil's musical ear shall have become somewhat blunted through being assailed, throughout those early stages, by incorrect and ugly tones. The other danger, which is more serious, is that his musical bent may have lost something of its right preoccupations and powers, because of disproportionate attention to the manipulative act; and the result of this may be that the musician that is produced will be one of those whose music appears to reside mainly in his fingers, and there only while the fingers are in motion. Both of these dangers are, moreover, in some degree inescapable, no matter what the method of teaching. However, good teaching can reduce both to an astonishingly small minimum; and it is safe to say that the amount of such reduction provides an unsurpassed criterion for evaluating the work of any teacher.

Tonal concepts for the vocalist

Now the dangers that have been described do not present themselves at all to the vocalist. In direct contrast the vocalist, theoretically speaking, may, and almost must, approach his tones as pure tonal images. It is painfully evident, however, that he has thus far failed to do so; and the reason is that, although he is immune to the dangers that confront the instrumentalist, he encounters others peculiar to his own field that are equally formidable and that have been equally deterrent.

The first danger for the vocalist, then, is one that arises from what appears to be a signal advantage: namely, that with his instrument he does not have to acquire a technique of producing tones, but finds himself in possession of a ready-made technique that works with unexampled facility. Thence comes, however, his fatal tendency to perform by ear. Instrumentalists have long been impatient with vocalists because they will not learn to read, and must be taught so largely by imitation. That he should learn to read is not too much to ask of the vocalist; but it is more than the instrumentalist thinks he is asking. What would the instrumentalist do with respect to reading if a fluent technique existed in him from the beginning? Would he not hesitate, as the vocalist has done, to interrupt its flow and force it to pick off notes, one at a time, from the staff?

Only because he has had to build up a technique of production, one note at a time, has the instrumentalist learned his staff-technique so perfectly. At every step it provided notes as fast as he could produce them. Had it been otherwise he would probably have turned away from it. In fact, as a singer he probably did turn from it, and to this day can not sing at sight any better than the vocalist; or at least he can not sing at sight with anything like the degree of facility with which he can play at sight.

But when the singer proceeds wholly and permanently on the basis of learning by imitation—which the public school teacher of music should strive mightily to prevent—he deprives his mind of a certain measure of its power to conceive tones, and of a musical development that comes only from conjuring tones out of their ideal world. The instrumentalist, at the moment when he is producing a tone, and perhaps as a result of the familiar action that does produce it and that so comes to predict it, does, at least for the moment, conceive it. But the vocalist, with no conscious process to prompt conception, is likely to become wholly receptive to tonal percepts from without rather than generative of tonal concepts from within; and if sheer imitation is thus too long his sole mode of response, his faculty of tonal ideation becomes barren. His only safety in that case lies in the fact that he does remember tones—he has to, since he does not read—and consequently does reflect on music, once it is in his head, probably more than does even the player.

The second obstacle that has prevented the vocalist from dealing with music in the tonal-conceptual way we have described has been his absorption with textual meanings and with emotions arising out of these, rather than absorption with the aesthetic object itself. This latter, of course, is the song *as* song; that is to say, it is the song considered as an art-product that must be viewed as a self-sufficient entity, a unity in itself, and that must not be passed over as having value only because it is supposed to be accessory to something quite outside itself. That fallacy fixes the attention and the affectionate remembrance of the singer's mind on an object other than its proper one, and on one which is outside the world of music altogether.

Removing dangers

So it would appear that if the instrumentalist has tended to become mechanically and practically musical, the vocalist has tended to become more vaguely musical. Both of them would be saved—and many have been and are being saved, day after day—by learning to conceive music abstractly, as the composer conceives it. Not but that it is even then conceived in terms of some particular medium of expression. It cannot become wholly abstract without becoming too pallid and too remote from sensation to stir us. Nevertheless, if we would lift music to its highest level, its abstract significance must be paramount; which is to say that when tonal ideas gain their significance and interest wholly by relationships within their own realm, they must be intrinsically more musical than when they acquire significance by various borrowings. Moreover, when they are thus more truly musical, they will perhaps be also of greater value in education; for the distinctive worth of music is found precisely in this, that it dwells more nearly in a realm of pure ideality than does any other mind-stuff; and it has untold value for an objective-minded people to-day for that very reason.

To conceive music thus abstractly means, for the vocalist, simply to conceive vocal tone instrumentally. As an agency for making music, the voice then becomes an instrumentality subject to none of the mechanistic dangers inherent in the true mechanical instrument, but for that very reason under the necessity of summoning music out of the purely conceptual and subjective realm rather than drawing it out of the sensory and objective world. The music so summoned, since it cannot be conceived entirely apart from the nature of the instrumentality that must voice it, will still have a distinctive style, just as music for the violin, or for the piano, must have a distinctive style. But that is not to say that in contrast to instrumental music it will be song, or will even be vocal music, in the sense previously imparted to the term. Rather it will now be simply pure music or absolute music, but conceived as for the voice, rather than as for viols or pipes; and it will consequently bear upon its image fewer marks of corporeal bondage than any other conceived music can show, excepting only that which may be born in the mind of the composer. In short, we would have in this new vocal music merely another style of instrumental music, but one that fortunately is of peculiarly abstract quality.

Singing without accompaniment

Now the unaccompanied chorus particularly when it sings music of true *a cappella* style, becomes a powerful agency for developing the pure type of musicianship described. No matter what the style of music sung, the absence of an accompaniment serves to promote tonal thinking, because the possibility of a short circuit from ear-sensation to voice-imitation is removed. The poor quality of that unpremeditated type of response can be proven in a moment by having a chorus sing very promptly after a brief "pitch"-chord is given. The ensuing tone is likely to be poor in quality and uncertain in intonation. At best it will be comparatively unmusical. On the other hand,[1] if the pitch is quietly sounded, and if then an interval of intense silence is granted, the tone will become mentally imaged during the hush, and a free, true, musical tone will come forth. But if this is true of the first chord, it is true in a measure of all those that follow; and the measure in which it is true depends upon the degree of expectedness, the amount of prefigured flow, that succeeding tones may or may not possess. In any case, however, an accompaniment tends to encourage slovenly tone-thinking and a habit of careless imitation; and, if it duplicates the voice-parts some-

[1] See Chapter IX: *Developing Musical Power.*

what persistently, the singer may finally descend to parrot-like reproduction of what is given him from moment to moment.

In contrast, unaccompanied choral music throws the singer upon his tonal memory and powers of tonal imagery. Even though the music is learned by rote, it does this eventually; and the eventuality is never so far distant that it can long be disregarded. Thus, although the composition has been learned by rote, and although in final performance the initial chord is strongly sounded on piano, the singer is from that moment deserted. No voice will speak further from the pianistic prompter's box, to keep him on the key or to direct him to some difficult interval. Instead of being alert to sensations from without he must accordingly become alert to promptings from within. If it be objected that he still must be alert to the other voices—as, indeed, he must—the answer is that these do not disturb his mental set so seriously. One reason for their less distracting objectivity is their similar quality of tone; and another is that they lack the jangling and exciting quality of tone of either the piano or the orchestra, due to the comparative absence from voice of numerous and diverse upper partials that are produced by instruments. The nature of the attack on tone by instruments is in general productive of further difference. Adjustment of vocal pitch to the lead from instruments is consequently marked usually by a greater sensory response, in proportion to conceptual effort, than is adjustment to the lead of other voices.

Different types of unaccompanied choral music

If unaccompanied choral music is of the descriptive or dramatically emotional order—as, for instance, is much of the striking Russian and Ukrainian music so marvelously sung for us by groups of singers native to those regions— the dramatic intention, together with the frequent introduction, also, of instrumental rhythms, might presumably shift the preoccupation of the singers away from the field of tonal concepts. That it does not, in the case of the groups referred to, is due to the fact that, in the absence of instruments that might provide accompaniments, their peoples have for ages made their vocal music complete and satisfying in itself, by extemporizing parts that are often richly elaborate. Few other nationalities, it is true, betray any such predisposition toward harmonic and contrapuntal complexities in their folk-music; and it may be that in this case it represents superiority in native musical ability rather than a particularly favorable experience. In any case, the tangential tendencies that may be prompted by the qualities of style under discussion are revealed when one attempts to develop an American chorus by means of a repertory of such music. Any director who would make that attempt would quickly discover that good performance of such music represents a high attainment rather than a process of training; and he learns that if he would most successfully train the voices, the ears, and the musical minds of his chorus, he must begin with music of quite different character.

That other music is found in the true *a cappella* field, or in slow-moving secular, and perhaps *romantic,* compositions, that may have distinct mood but that are not fervidly emotional. Pieces that might appropriately be played on the organ, or by a small group of strings, or by a choir of brass instruments, are in point. But this is equivalent to saying that the music should partake largely of the character, and should fulfill largely the function, of instrumental music, whether that be of classic or romantic type. In truth, this is precisely what all of the best of unaccompanied choral music does, and does primarily, even though it adds at the same time something that no group of instruments could give. Proof of this is found in the singing of the Russian choirs referred to; for even while they sing the most songful and dramatic of part-songs, and perhaps particularly while they sing that very kind, they seek, by getting extraordinary tone-colors in their voices, and tone-colors that frequently resemble those of musical instruments, to impart pure tonal charm, interest, and variety to what, on casual thought, would appear to be little but ordinary "song-story" material. What they add to song, in short, is sheer musicalness, that at once glorifies it beyond its literalness.

Possible values in a cappella *singing*

If the right repertory and the right mode of instruction can be supplied, unaccompanied choral singing may easily become the most potent agency we can have in our schools

for developing a peculiarly thorough and refined musicianship, and also for building an education and culture that
will rest, as all education and culture must, upon dealings
with ideas stored in the mind rather than with reactions
to sensations impinging from without. More will be said
on this point in a later chapter. Since that later phase of
our discussion deals, however, with the musical psychology
of the individual, it remains here and now to make some
further comparisons of vocal with instrumental music in
their objective aspects, not only with reference to the characteristics of the music produced, but also with reference
to the machinery of its production.

Chorus and orchestra: their music

Compared with one another, the chorus is simple and
frugal, the orchestra is complex and lavish. In the one are
from three or four to eight or ten parts; the other has from
sixteen parts, or twenty-three parts (as in the classical orchestra of the Viennese period) up to some forty parts. The few
parts in the chorus moreover tend comparatively to a uniformity of tone-color such as exists in the orchestra in the
string section or in the brass section alone; but in the different sections of the orchestra is a diversity of tone-color, that
makes of it a many-hued rainbow, for which no match can
be found in the chorus. The many voices and parts of the
orchestra are individualized, too, not only by differences
in tone-color, but by different capacities with respect to
rhythm and phrasing. The trumpet differs from the flute

as much in the character of the rhythms appropriate to it
as in its tone-color. Rhythmically the instruments of the
orchestra, as we found earlier, speak more sharply and de-
cisively than do voices; and the percussions are present to
provide incomparably pungent rhythmic punctuation, when
such accentuation is wanted. The temper of the vocal tone,
too, is cool and quiet, although definite, indubitable, and
strong; the orchestral tone, on the contrary, is brilliant,
warm, exciting, and, if need be, riotous. It could not be
otherwise when instruments with many different systems
of upper-partials speak at once. In tonal range, too, the
orchestra is prodigal, the chorus restricted; and in agility
various instruments of the orchestra surpass even the most
phenomenal of voices. Moreover, in extremely rapid passages the tones from instruments remain distinct, while in
the voice they merge or blur into one another.

But against all of this may be urged one simple reflection,
namely, that prodigality of resource was never yet the condition or guarantee of supremacy in art. Indeed, it may even
prove a hindrance to the highest artistic attainment. The
very opulence of the orchestra gives it a power to overcome our senses before, and whether or not, it convinces
our spirits. Purity, simplicity, and restraint, which are not
the orchestra's characteristic charms, are as highly and
wholly transporting as a riot of color and weaving line.
For art is a matter of balance and proportion within the
medium. Thus it happens that the exquisite lines of a Gre-
cian urn may give us more joy than many an elaborate de-

sign, and that a sketch in black and white may surpass in life-giving power a multitude of polychrome paintings; and thus it happens, too, that Palestrina, with a few bare voices, can lift us in ecstasy to a point higher in heaven than that to which the grand sonorities of Wagner's *Parsifal* can carry us. Where we gain in sensation, indeed, we are likely to lose in abstract, spiritual significance. The Almighty need not vociferate. After the tumult of wind came a still, small voice. From the standpoint of its cultural power we need not, therefore, distrust the efficacy of the *a cappella* chorus. We must, however, be wise enough to seek its characteristic values, and not try to make it compete with orchestral values, or with the values of the operatic chorus, on their own grounds. If we do that we will but fail, and will at the same time show ourselves aesthetically obtuse.

Chorus and orchestra: their performers

The reaction of playing upon the player has been in part discussed. It would be interesting, perhaps, to discuss in much the same way the reaction of singing upon the singer. That it is vastly different we know from both observation and experience; and the difference in such subjective re-actions is of first importance in any educational inquiry. Nevertheless, an inquiry into the physiological and mental reactions of the individual singer does not promise to be fruitful enough to justify the effort; and moreover, were we to be thorough, we should need also to investigate the reactions experienced from playing the piano as compared with the harp, the oboe as compared with the violin, or the trombone as compared with the bassoon. There does appear to be a different subjective reaction in each case; but the reaction to music in general, or to music in the abstract, appears to be so much greater and so much more important that it dwarfs the smaller inquiry.

But in the mass, participants in chorus and in orchestra undergo two different types of training and experience, and these, we may conjecture, tend to leave different attitudes and dispositions in the members. Whether this is actually so or not would be difficult to prove, because individuals in either group differ greatly among themselves, and the personalities of the conductors or teachers are very influential. Nevertheless, an analysis of the differences in the two experiences will be helpful to the teacher, whether tangible effects are definitely measurable or not.

One difference that affects the musical atmosphere of rehearsals of the two kinds of organization is the comparative quiet and simplicity of the choral gathering. Chairs and music stands must be placed for the orchestra; the distribution of music is a considerable task, since all members do not receive uniform parts; and moreover, setting up and warming up instruments, and tuning them, creates some confusion and distraction. From almost all of this practical detail the singers are relieved; and a social rather than a business-like air consequently pervades the preparations for a chorus practice. But after the rehearsal begins, and, indeed, at every point in their experience, the players are still called into a measure of contact with the practical, the organized, the mechanistic, which may be small as compared with the contacts required of men in non-musical pursuits, but is yet wholly beyond any demands of the kind that are laid upon the singer. Most instruments are quite intricate tools, and their mechanical condition is consequently a matter of practical concern. Strings break; bows lose hair; reeds "go bad"; valves stick; temperatures affect tunings. The singer may grow hoarse or may acquire a sore throat; but that is a personal disability, not a mechanical problem. Is it because of such correlations that singers as a class are a bit less practical and efficient in small details than orchestra or band musicians?

The singer is ordinarily less responsible than the player. In calling joint rehearsals of a chorus and orchestra, the conductor may expect punctual arrival of the players rather than of the singers; and of the singers, sopranos will be more tardy than altos. This last fact is not to be explained. But as to the sense of responsibility displayed by orchestra players, as compared with singers, the explanation may lie in the fact that, except for members of the string section, each member of the orchestra has an individual part, which will be lacking, and probably very conspicuously lacking, if he is not there to play it. In a chorus, on the other hand, there are dozens of members to sustain any one part from which one singer may be absent; so why should he be present every moment?

Finally, singing is a natural emotional expression, unchecked by any chill indirection of performance. Indeed, more premeditation is what we have been urging upon the singer. The instrumentalist, on the other hand, deals in precisions and mechanisms, and may grow cold through too much calculation and precisionism in his action; but the singer may remain somewhat impulsive because so little calculation and precisely manipulated action is needed. Of course, this applies chiefly to the solo singer, rather than to the singer in a chorus, and especially the singers of the kind of music described as appropriate to the *a cappella* chorus. But in all singing there is great vital stimulus and warmth as compared with most playing; and this, coupled with the emotional expression, gives the vocalists a more acute sense of generous well-being and emotional vigor than that which is normally generated in the player.

All in all, then, the singer tends to become somewhat more impulsive, more sociable, more expansive, and perhaps more human, than the player; and the player tends to become more rational, more practical, more precise and responsible, and perhaps less warm-hearted, than the singer. The more, however, that both singing and playing are brought into the service of high and specifically musical ideals, the more do these diversities tend to disappear; and in the end, if both pursue their highest functions, instruments and voices will lose their superficial diverse aspects, and alike will serve a common cause in a common musical language.

CHAPTER FOURTEEN

The Creative Element in Education

The word 'creative' is being much used of late in educational discussions. We hear of creative thought, creative projects, creative teaching, creative learning, creative supervision. In particular, the progressives in education employ the word frequently; but they are also doing an inestimable service to the cause of education in America by intelligently and ardently putting creative education into effect. Generally, however, there has been little sharp definition of the meaning of 'creative,' as used in the foregoing connections, and probably the term is but vaguely connotative to many persons who use it. Before we discuss the creative idea in application to teaching music, we will accordingly make some inquiry as to the nature of creative action in general.

All mental activity is creative

It will help us, perhaps, if we begin with the reflection that all mental processes other than the most mechanical reactions—and these hardly rise to the threshold of the conscious at all, and so may not be exceptions—are inescapably creative. This fact, affirmed by philosophers, and by psychologists who are other than physiologists with psychological leanings, underlies the philosophy of the entire first division of this book. It takes for granted that no percept is merely a mechanical registration upon a brain, but is also something that is appropriated by, and colored to the preferences and interests of, an individual; and it thus becomes a factor in that "coordinated maintenance" of which Haldane spoke. Each personality will therefore continue to be distinct, precisely because, obeying some principle of individuation within itself, it will transmute the percepts that become lodged in it into something that other organisms cannot possibly duplicate. And in this principle of individuation, in the fact that mechanical equivalents, as objectively perceived, do not produce uniform or predictable results, is seen that creative character which Bergson and others recognize as the distinguishing mark of the human mind.

Some aspects of mechanical learning

Now the phase of education that concerns itself with mechanical learning, while it cannot prevent individuation, is likely to disregard the creative character of mind, and the desirability of giving it play by allowing education to acquire a distinctive, individual character. Reproductive memory, made dependable by a vast amount of repetition and mechanical drill, is rather its reliance. The use of such memory is expected to instruct the pupils finally to such good effect that they can all return precisely the same answers to certain stated inquiries. That is to say, education

from this point of view is assumed to consist in the acquisition of a body of incontrovertible facts; and the test
of its success, since the facts do not change during the
process of their acquisition, is the measure of uniformity
attained in the answers. Within limits the protagonists of
this view are, of course, correct. Indisputably there is a
fundament of facts—for instance, those of the multiplication table—which do not vary, which should become the
property of all, and concerning which no original opinions
or interpretations are wanted. So regarded, the theory of
knowledge-inculcation is not faulty; but if it appears unobjectionable at this point by reason of what it affirms, we
may still find it far from unobjectionable, at another point,
in what it omits.

One shortcoming of the fact-learning theory is the assumption, implied to some extent in it, that the end of the
educational effort has been attained, at least for the teacher
and the school, when the facts have been learned. Conceding that they should be learned, one must still recognize
that the method of learning them, the interest-attitudes
created in the student, and the preferences developed in
him that will result in the choice of the path in which
he will utilize the facts learned, are by far the more important considerations. In a slightly different way, the fact-
learning conception of education may again be seen to be
faulty because what is to be learned has no value except
that which it acquires in terms of usefulness and significance in the mind of the learner; and that value is pred-

icated upon the learner's interest, his capacity to deal with
the knowledge gained, and his tendency to exercise that
capacity in ways that appear to him rewarding. If these
values are not present—and they are neglected in mechanical learning—it is difficult to see how knowledge in the
learner's head is in any way better than it would be if
left on call in the encyclopedia.

Creative education in contrast

Now the chief characteristic of the creative education
outlook is that it attaches value primarily to the learner,
and is consequently more concerned with the individual
development that accrues to him through his grasp on and
use of the knowledge and experience gained, than it is with
the amount and logical organization of the factual content
that may be stored mechanically but not used. That is to
say, creative education places emphasis upon energy and
vitality of mental functioning, and upon individuation as
a condition of vitality, rather than upon the fruits of mental
functioning; or, figuratively speaking, it regards the manner and effect of playing the game as of more importance
than the size of the score. There is danger, of course, that
just as undue emphasis upon mechanical learning may lead
to disregard of the free development of the mind and personality, so undue emphasis upon that free development
may lead to disregard for learning, when that is conceived
as mastery of the formal content of a curricular subject.
But advantage would appear, on the whole, to lie with the

proponents of human development; for abundant volitional activity is likely to lead in the end to some worthy attainment, and so to gain both goals; while attainment without volition does not at all surely presage any result beyond itself. Only when there is volitional life, in other words, is there hope.

Creative education as developmental of individuality

We see, then, that self-directed activity of the mind, as distinguished from the mechanical knowledge-storing process, represents a search, a thrust of the mind, for knowledge or discovery; that this thrust takes the direction of individual interest and preference; and, it cannot be too emphatically said, this preference, in turn, represents *a sure instinct toward the fulfillment of a purpose that in essence is the maintenance and development of the individuality.* It is, in short, for each personality, a search for that which will develop and nurture that particular personality. This does not imply that the whole curriculum should be thrown away and that the separate individuals should be left to forage at large in the vast world of things and ideas. Individualities are not so diverse that unlike worlds are needed for them. The human race is of one species, and all persons are alike interested in much the same things. But it does imply that subtle and minute, but potent, differentiations of interest about any one *thing* exist in different individuals. Not the amount of interest, then, but especially this particular direction and peculiar cast of it, are differentiated.

Even the multiplication table is not recited in the same tone of voice by different pupils, and does not have the same connotations to all. "Four," may mean yards to the track-man, dollars to the commercial student, measures and a musical phrase to the musical pupil.

By the principal of individuation, the knowledge that each stores up from infancy thus acquires an individual character. Environment and experience will have much to do with the gross product, but the utmost uniformity in these will not produce like uniformity in the individuals who respond to them. The differentiation becomes progressive, too, first because the already acquired content has a directive influence upon future attention and interest, and secondly, because, even when new experience is not thus selected, it must still be assimilated into an already specially formed apperceptive background.

Mechanical learning in contrast

The individual cast of interest, that makes each individual translate any uncolored fact into terms of special meaning and preference, is often either ignored or unwisely treated in education. Mechanism disregards coloration. Being of objectivist faith, it discerns no colorations in facts and anticipates none in individuals. Learning then becomes a discipline, to be mechanically pursued in subserviency or in cold-blooded determination. If teacher-domination is added, personal attitude may even become an offense. For the individual pupil, deprived of the opportunity to discover his own avenues of approach to a subject, may have no slightest spring of his interest touched, and may thereupon appear uncompliant, if not refractory. The downright hostility sometimes shown by pupils toward learning, even in connection with subjects that have natural attractiveness, is doubtless attributable to this quality of inflexibility that is imposed upon both the subject-matter and the modes of response left open to the pupils. And if this is so, any amount of thought and effort might well be expended in devising a plan by which the child could be led into interested and whole-souled cooperation in the educational adventure at hand.

General features of creative education

Now creative education provides such a plan. It does not require a chaotic jumbling of subject-matter, nor does it require that each teacher teach only one pupil at a time, in order to respect his individuality. It conceives, rather, a mode of learning that is to be pursued by all alike, at the same time, and in connection with any and every subject. It does not seek to make individuals diverse, but rather tends to weld them together in sympathetic understanding and cooperation. It does this, not by endeavoring to lodge different subject-matters in different heads, but by giving every mind opportunity to lay hold on any chosen bit of subject-matter by allowing it to reach for that subject-matter with the particular sort of prehensile apparatus (so to speak) with which *it* happens to be equipped. For no two minds, as we have said, approach any experience from precisely the same angle, or with the same set of mind, or with the same orientation of interest and feeling. In fact, any experience is not quite the *same* experience to two different minds. Creative education gives heed to this fact, and permits the minds of all pupils to play over the various aspects of the given problem in such way that each finds the point on which it may settle, and from which it may move on to explore the remainder of the problem.

Some dangers of the method

Now the method, remedial though it is of certain ills, leads to some types of result that are disquieting when compared with the results achieved by means of formal instruction, and against which the teacher long accustomed to formal procedures must be fortified. Instead of all pupils responding in like manner, the response of each will now be subtly different from all the others. This does not mean the facts will be altered: the multiplication table will still stand. It does imply, however, that possibly no two pupils will be dealing with precisely the same facts at the same moment, and that all will perhaps have to pool their findings in order to complete the enterprise. Such pooling represents, indeed, the "sympathetic cooperation" lately alluded to—which is so much better than a demand for identical results. It implies, further, one departure that often disturbs the experimenting teacher: namely, a logical ordering and grading of facts will possibly be tossed aside by the unruly spring freshets of creative action. Entering the field at various salients, it is inevitable that the minds of the pupils will encounter problems somewhat out of their logical turn.

The teacher may feel that there is an element of loss in this; but there are compensating reflections. One is that the flow of interest and energy that results from freedom to select the path of approach is life-giving; the pupils become their own teachers. Another is that logical organization may reasonably take place, without disadvantage, after all the facts are in, instead of keeping step with the facts as they come, and marshaling them in—or, perhaps we should say, doling them out. Indeed we may reflect that systemization of facts after they are all in—and usually somewhat haphazardly garnered—is the law of most of our education, except for that part of it which we gather in the schoolroom. And the results are not altogether unfortunate. Against all disadvantages that inhere in the mode must be weighed the fact that knowledge acquired in such order has at least, at every step of the way, a significance and usableness often denied the items under the logical plan of purveyance. For creative learning pursues the order of interest and of personal mental need, and not the order of external articulation. And when we say this, we are saying that knowledge gained *out of* the *logical* order is very likely to be knowledge gained *in* the *psychological* order.

The difference in results which is most frequently pointed out, is that under creative teaching the uniform, standard-

ized, product that is characteristic of mechanical methods
is supplanted by a product each item of which is original,
different, unique. Now, doubt often arises in the pedagogical mind as to whether such difference, instead of being a
virtue, is not rather symptomatic of comparative laxity and
weakness. And in truth it may be. Under creative methods
the teacher is constantly faced with the possibility that hasty
products of superficial and irresponsible mind-wanderings
may be proffered as "creative"; and the "creative" teacher,
if not somewhat strong in technique and profound in understanding, may be moved to accept the feeble and meaningless offerings with altogether misplaced satisfaction, on
the ground that they are at least "original." But such a bar-
gain is not good enough; it is hardly fair to offer only weak
and capricious stirrings of original thought in exchange for
the solid—even if comparatively lifeless—output of mech-
anized learning. Creative education must thus guard against
flabbiness, even as mechanical instruction must guard
against ossification. Only if the pupils can be deeply
aroused, and be led to become progressively ever more en-
grossed and absorbed, can creative education be fully
justified.

Requisites for success

To achieve the full end of creative education, it is necessary that the teacher have far more pedagogical wisdom
than is essential to success in mechanical instruction. The
subject-matter must be held up in a new light—in a thous-

and new lights. It is no longer to be a restricted thing, existent in a book and within the walls of a schoolroom, but it is to become a part of life, with all the connections and meanings, the ramifications and the varied hues, that it has in a world outside the schoolroom. Those ramifications, hues, and meanings it has acquired in the world because there it has long been the property of countless human minds, all different, who have shaped it to their interests and uses. They have had freedom; they have taken a content and moulded and adapted it; and they still continue so to do.

But the tyranny of the schoolroom is in the fact that subject-matter there is ordinarily fixed and unyielding, and can not be moulded to satisfy individual appetites and needs. The escape is to permit it to be flexible, to have countless aspects. Those aspects exist potentially in the understanding of the versatile-minded teacher; and the teacher knows that they are the aspects which the subject may assume in the minds of all the pupils collectively. All of the guises and hues it may wear, she does not and can not know. The pupils will disclose them in unexpected variety when at last given opportunity. And the opportunity is afforded whenever the pupils are invited to lay hold on the subject-matter and mould it to *their* uses, instead of being used themselves (as they ordinarily feel they are) in the service of an unyielding subject-matter that never reciprocates.

Finally, *the creative project provides the agency by which the subject may thus be made to serve them.* But it must truly serve them, they must have freedom to use it in *their* ways, if deep interest and response, and true originality and rich self-development are to result. The feeble and insincere product, that represents only superficial mind-wanderings, may possibly be the product of individuals who have not yet found their own uses for the stuff of the creative project, but it is more likely to come from pupils who have been led to work toward the production of some pattern that was in the mind of the teacher rather than in their own minds. Only when they have full freedom, after a wise preview has been given them, can depth and authenticity of response be confidently expected of them.

CHAPTER FIFTEEN

Creative Thought in Music

In an earlier chapter of this book [1] the discussion centered
on auditory imagery. In the present chapter we wish to
discuss the action of the mind in its dealings with such
imagery. This action, in so far as it goes beyond reproductive memory, appears to possess all the characteristics that
would ordinarily identify it as thought; and certain forms
of it are moreover distinguished by special aspects which
would ordinarily be accepted as marking the presence of
creative thought. Since, however, these two terms are often
somewhat loosely used, and in order, moreover, to make
perfectly clear the outlook from which creative music will
herein be discussed, we shall describe explicitly the mental
processes themselves, as we conceive them. Whether or not
the reader then wishes to accept the terms we apply to them
he can decide without interruption of the inquiry.

Percepts and memory

Following Meumann, we discussed learning from the
standpoint of imprinting. That is learned which is im-
printed in memory. This view emphasizes the place of

[1] Chapter IX: *Developing Musical Power.* The reader is advised, at this point,
to review it briefly.

exact, reproductive memory. It gives an entirely reliable account of a form of memory, and consequently of learning, upon which great weight is placed in most of our modern, educational endeavors, and which leads, in an impoverished form of development, to the mechanical type of learning that was described in our preceding chapter. It need not, it is true, descend to quite such a mechanistic plane as was there described, for aesthetic as well as factual interest may invest the experience—at least in the case of music—and so relieve the memory of its otherwise wholly arid, mechanistic character. But at best the memory invoked, whether held in affection in the mind, or whether wholly schematic and cold, was assumed to be a replica of the original percept.

And so, in a sense, it is. We must note in passing, however, that a memory of a percept, no matter how faithfully it represents the original is not the same thing as the percept itself. Bergson [1] puts the distinction well when he states: "The memory seems to be to the perception what the image reflected in the mirror is to the object in front of it. The object can be touched as well as seen; acts on us as well as we on it; is pregnant with possible actions; it is *actual*. The image is *virtual,* and though it resembles the object, it is incapable of doing what the object does."

Now this distinction applies, as we have said, to the most accurate reproductions. Of more importance to our inquiry, however, is the measure of fidelity of images to the

[1] *Mind-Energy:* Henri Bergson.

original percept, and the question of the importance of such fidelity, or the lack of it, in any case. Henderson [1] discusses this question admirably, but his discussion is too extended to lend itself to our purposes here. A mere skeleton outline is all that we can now offer; and this will have to be bent quickly to apply only to music.

To begin, then, a sensation, in some mysterious way, evokes or gives rise to a percept. The after-image, as when we gaze at a glowing electric bowl, and immediately after close our eyes, is precisely this percept—or shall we, for convenience, wrongly say this sensation?—reproduced. The after-image in itself, we should note, is sensational. It has in it all the sharpness, the compelling power, of the sensation itself.

Reproductive memory and imagery

Now no memory has the character of an after-image. Almost immediately the image, though we strive to recall it in its perceptional fullness and potency, loses not only its sharp perceptional tang, but also lapses from its original completeness. It becomes spectral and uncertain in detail. But lest we begin to regret this as though it were a mental weakness, let us observe that meanwhile there has been no slightest loss in the *general* aspect of the image, nor in its *significance and meaning*. Indeed, only when the disturbing imperativeness of sensation has departed from the experience, are we able to comprehend it with respect to its sig-

[1] *A Textbook in the Principles of Education:* Ernest Norton Henderson.

nificance. So long as it is a sensation, its details are stamped upon our sensorium without our participation, so to speak, and therefore apart from the exercise of our powers of discrimination. The function of sensation, indeed, would seem to be thus to present undiscriminated raw material to the mind. *But it does not and can not remain undiscriminated.* At the very moment of perception an image may be formed; and since any image is also a memory, Bergson is justified in speaking of this image that accompanies perception as a *memory of the present.* And any such image, coincident or later (except the after-image, which need not here be distinguished from the perception itself), immediately discloses deviations from literal reproduction that move it from the realm of sensation into the realm of preferential interpretation, or, in a word, move it into the world of idea. And this movement is characterized, so to speak, by a dropping of excess baggage (of literal detail), and a preserving of essential or selected features only. Perception itself is made the clearer by thus being relieved of the irrelevant and confusing. As Henderson [1] states: "The process of distortion involved in reproductive imagination, so far from being a mere falling away from the accuracy and clearness of perception, is in point of fact a very important condition of greater clearness and accuracy, not only in ideas, but also in perceptions themselves. . . . The interpretations that in their original fusion with sensation were

[1] *Op. cit.*

vague and unanalyzed become clear-cut and ideational in quality. . . . Perception acquires a background."

Memory for technical use

The aim of this discussion has been to make clear the distinction between reproductive memory and the imagination and reflection that ordinarily take place in the mind. Before we elaborate, however, on the latter, in application to music, it is necessary to note one particular use of strictly reproductive memory that is of interest to the educator. Whenever technical action by the individual is involved, the literal reproductive imagination will be found necessary; and it is worthy of remark that this is but another aspect of the fact that the rational intellect has to do with our action upon the objective world. Applying the thought to music, for instance, it is not sufficient for the extemporizing accompanist, when the music is lost, to remember the mood and rhythm of the melody in general: a complete reproductive memory is needed instead. In fact, whenever we would read notes, write notes, sing or play, we must deal in precisions. In all these technical actions, therefore, as in all technical action in every field, we find ourselves returning repeatedly to the original experience, to check once more the accuracy of our perceptions and to correct our errors and shortcomings. Lest this should appear, however, a superior, and perhaps the only proper, mode of mental functioning, let us reflect that a mind that contained nothing but these precise reproductions would obviously be caught up in the completed and the proffered, from which it could never escape to discoveries and original actions of its own. Such a mind would in reality be dead—a sarcophagus for the reception of records that could not know they existed—and such an organism would be an imitative automatom. Yet we must note that creative thought, which is of vastly different nature, leads immediately to technical processes, and therefore to the necessity for exact reproductive memory; and the two kinds of mental action, involving two types or two stages of imagery, are therefore constantly needed, and will inevitably alternate and interpenetrate in any musical activity that is more than idle musing on one hand, or stark mechanics on the other.

Auditory imagery for creative use

With respect to music, then, and with respect to creative dealings with it, the auditory imagery that may and does come to haunt the mind must be seen, not as a collection of literal records of certain songs, scales, or other specific tonal productions, such as are needed for technical purposes, but as a reservoir of musical elements that have attained flexibility for creative groupings by detachment from specificity. Such ideas are abstractions, precisely as our idea of a tree is not an image of any one tree that we ever saw, yet is formed by abstraction of elements from any or every tree. That such auditory imagery, holding promise of the possibility of creative instead of wholly imitative dealings with music, exists in every normal mind in some degree has not been sufficiently recognized. Indeed, that such imagery, bearing such promise, exists in minds in connection with every field of human interest, and has not been sufficiently recognized by educators, is the contention of progressive educational leaders to-day. They may not so analyze it, it is true, but they do declare in favor of creative teaching and creative learning.

And from our point of view creative, as contrasted with mechanical learning, can have no meaning except as it implies psychologically a transfer from the field of the literal image—for knowledge—to the field of the significant idea—for understanding. Of course the transfer is only a shift in emphasis, since it is quite impossible wholly to repress the growth of ideas, on the one hand, or wholly to suppress the desire and necessity for exact knowledge, on the other; but the shift is nevertheless of the nature described. It has long been delayed in music, partly because of absorption with exacting technical demands, partly because of a lack of faith in the musical endowments of the average person, and to some extent, perhaps, because of the hope that music would prove re-creative, if not creative, and would thus escape the evils attendant upon mechanistic processes. But observation proves that in practice the re-creative function does not fully offset the evils arising from the mechanical processes that are also followed; and the understanding and appreciation sought through creative methods are therefore not developed.

As to the fear that musical endowments are lacking in

the rank and file, one may reply that they merely have not been disclosed because methods of teaching did not invoke them. A little experimenting, however, will convince the teacher that a wealth of musical ideas does exist in the minds of children generally, and will spring into eager life as soon as opportunity is given. Indications of the fact have abounded, too, and why we should have been blind to them is inexplicable: for children croon before they speak, and improvise hummings and carolings and whistlings throughout all their years. That they should then be restricted, in educational practice, wholly to the reproduction, in imagination and in fact, of given models, appears to be as regrettable a blunder, in kind if not in results, as it would be were they similarly restricted in the use of word-language.

Improvisation as thought

The creative activity in music which would appear to be most essentially educational in terms of music is that which was alluded to in an earlier chapter as characterizing the work of the composer. Improvisation of melodies by school children—later entailing notation, of course—is accordingly the form of creative activity that has been considered or implied throughout this entire discussion. Other types of creative activity in music exist, and have been highly developed in various schools, but there is no need to analyze them here. They can be interpreted and evaluated in the light of the general analysis of mental processes that has already been set down. We have yet, however, to examine creative activity, as it appears in the improvisation of melodies and of extended works, with reference to certain further aspects. And these have to do with its strength and worth as mental effort, as education in music, and finally, as developmental of individuality.

To refuse to creative musical activity of the kind specified the designation 'thought,' appears to the author to be quite indefensible. There has been, it is true, some tendency to restrict the application of the word 'thought' to efforts at problem-solving, or to rational efforts using scientific and mathematical data. The solving of a mathematical problem collectively by the children in a schoolroom would thus be held to require thought. The designing and fitting together of parts of metal or wood to make some machine or structure would likewise be held to require thought. If, however, the children should collectively create phrases of a melody and fit them together into a composition, although in this case even the original design would have to be conceived by them, and no part would be furnished them ready made, there would be a disposition on the part of some persons to speak of 'imagination' and 'feeling,' but to avoid the word 'thought.' Yet the mental processes in the three cases are identical: not the function, but the material upon which it is exercised alone differs. The material, in each case, would appear to be images and ideas resident in the mind; and the mental function would appear to be that grouping and comparing and shifting of them—that "thought-experimentation"—which we all know by experience, and which is normally continued until a satisfactory pattern is achieved. In the case of music, "justly called the most subjective of the arts," the fact that the mental process deals with images and ideas thus resident in the mind is quite evident.

In the case of preoccupation with a structure of wood or iron, the idealistic character of the stuff of thought is less likely to be discerned because of the obtrusiveness of the objective substance. Yet a little reflection makes it quite clear that all changes and reshapings and fittings that finally enter into the fashioning of the structure are not made in fact, but only in imaginative thought. There, and there almost wholly, is the completed product, and possibly every part of it separately, built, tried, torn down, altered, and rebuilt, again and again.

The construction of a good and expressive tune in no wise differs, therefore, from the construction of a model wind-mill, except that in the case of the latter tangible results, that can be objectively tested and measured, are to be attained, while in the case of the tune the result can be appraised only with reference to some shadowy ideal of fitness and perfection. But so far as thought is concerned, this gives superior value to the tune-making; for our physical senses may test the material structure when our conceptual power fails, while the worth of the tune, in the making of it and upon its completion, is gauged by reference to an immaterial and wholly conceptual standard that cannot be objectively displayed. The one structure must work; the other must satisfy. The less exacting and difficult task, so far as thought is concerned, is to make the thing that will work.

Thought and its materials

From the point we have now reached, thought follows sensation and perception, and deals with the subjective content that remains as a result of perception. Thought thus begins where learning—in the sense of acquiring the raw materials for thought—leaves off: the attention is focused outwardly in learning, inwardly in thinking. Applied to music, the subjective content offered for musical thought is not the tunes and stereotyped forms that have been learned and literally recorded, but is the store of musical ideas and images that have emerged from these through the constant selective, interpretive, organizing action of the mind. Mental dealings with these—comparing, rehearsing, combining, and transforming them—is thought, on the same terms that would make similar dealings with any other subjective content deserve the term: namely, the dealings must be purposive, and not be flaccid mind-wanderings. Strength and depth of thought are accordingly defined in terms of function, not of subject-matter; and dealings, with tonal materials may be as profoundly intellectual as dealings with mathematical abstractions.[1]

A Beethoven or a Bach is not less than an Edison or an Einstein, or than a Lloyd George or a Shakespeare. There is a generic resemblance, indeed, between all great men,

[1] See also Dewey, *How We Think*, Chapter III.

however diverse the fields may be in which their minds are exercised, and that resemblance is surely due precisely to the fact that the processes of thinking, the manner in which mental content is marshaled and mastered, and the capacity for this marshaling of the subjective resources, are always the same. All the great have the capacity for what may still be termed abstract thinking.

To think *music,* then, is to be as intellectual as to think *about* it, or as to think on staff-notation, or acoustic facts, or on any other non-tonal matters that cluster on the frontier or hide beneath the surface of music itself. And the only way to ensure activity of musical thought is to turn at times from the tones that are clamoring from without to the tonal voices that speak from within. Many teachers, and doubtless most children, remain unaware that they possess voices that speak from within. They remain objectively oriented with respect to music to the end of their days, and consequently do not become educated in music or through music. For once more it must be said, that while some mechanical learning may be gained through objectively focused attention, intellectual life does not begin until the external has been taken back of the tympanum and the retina into the retreats of the conceptual mind, there to become the focus of attention and thought.

Values of creative musical thought

Creative work in music—and it would be the same in any subject—is not only thus more deep and powerful in its intellectual aspects than is the mere process of "learning music," but it promises to contribute also toward the development of certain desirable qualities of personality and character that are untouched by the learning that proceeds too largely through mechanical processes. For that learning, as we have seen, tends toward standardization and uniformity, and any adequate process of education should develop on the part of the individual some measure, at least, of independent preference, knowledge of his own particular resources, ability to strike along original paths of thought, and reliance upon canons of judgment that he finds developed within himself. Now all real thought, as contrasted with mechanical learning, leads to these results; for all thought, at least as we have described it, is inevitably original and creative. Facts, as they are objectively regarded, are brutally unmodifiable; but images and ideas, as they develop in the mind, become plastic cognitive elements, plastic structural factors, that will inevitably be moulded into patterns and be sent forth into the world bearing insignia that will distinguish them from the products of any other individual whatsoever. And in thus producing, the producer finds himself, and in his product he sees himself. What he learns is not merely sterile subject-matter, but is the relation of that subject-matter to life, and his own relation to that subject-matter as an active element in life. Quoting from an earlier writing: "If we want men of conviction, men of independent critical ability, we must exercise and develop, and not deride, suppress, or regard condescendingly, the original impulses, dreams, and activities of children."

Specific musical values

Finally, the question will arise, in connection with a program of creative activity in music, whether it will not conflict with the attainment of that solid knowledge and skill that, regardless of other values that may be attained, are yet indispensable to a proper educational result. In the preceding chapter we admitted the possibility of such a shortcoming; but it is only a possibility, and it is but just to recognize that equal failure to develop a sound, formal knowledge of music, and power to deal competently with musical notation, may attend instructional endeavors that make no slightest effort toward any other achievement. If interest, taste, understanding, and enthusiasm are developed by creative education in music, and if, at the same time, knowledge of musical theory and ability to sing at sight should not be found conspicuously lacking, there would be small reason to condemn efforts in creative music.

But in theory, creative music should really strengthen, and not weaken, the development of knowledge and skill. With reference to reading music, for instance, it is evident that ability to interpret the notational symbols implies some conception of the musical ideas which they symbolize; and yet, at the same time, the ideas must remain hidden until interpretation of the symbols reveals them. Sight-reading thus becomes in a measure, for all except the musically ex-

pert, a groping for a meaning that is *hidden behind* symbols quite as surely as it is revealed by them. But under the
plan followed in creative music activities, this situation becomes reversed at the moment the pupils begin to notate
their songs. The musical idea, the meaning, now lies at the
outset clearly and attractively in the thought, and the notational symbols used to express it no longer appear as vague
or uncertain in meaning, but grow clear, definite, and eloquent. Theoretically, they should not lose that clear and
eloquent meaning when they are encountered in songs by
others in future days. Again, in reading songs by others,
tonal thinking is dulled because of the engagement of the
mind with the symbols behind which the tonal meaning
lurks. To some extent, notes are in the thought instead of
tones; and after the song is fully learned it is doubtful
whether its tones are recalled again and again with that
absorption in them, that attention to their every quality,
which would lead to the highest possible musical development. But when a song is born in the mind, precisely this
extraordinarily sensitive regard for its tones, this intense
preoccupation and reflection in connection with musical
ideas, takes place. Fine aural descrimination, excellent hearing, ability to think tones and deal with them, should therefore result from creative music processes.

Creative music tested

So the matter appears theoretically. Ordinary observation
of results attained in schools that have cultivated much

original composition has usually tended to confirm the favorable theoretical forecast. Lately, however, one carefully guarded experimental study has been made and results have been objectively measured, so far as such measurement is possible. The report, quoted entire in the appendix to this volume (at the cost, be it confessed, of some repetition) happily justifies the faith held by the supporters of creative activities in music.

We would add, in closing, one further reflection. As seen in its genesis in the mind, music is of the mental, the spiritual. But seen from this same standpoint, all that man produces, of a material as well as an immaterial nature, is likewise essentially mental or spiritual. For any human product, even the most insignificant, must first exist as idea: accidents of man's hands are not products, and in a real sense do not exist. So the creative character of all thought, which we affirmed at the beginning of this discussion, again is made evident.

It is a pity that education, fastening its attention upon the sensuous world which furnishes the material upon which the mind is to play, and which it is the function of the mind to interpret and organize for the benefit of the mind and personality and spirit, should have come to regard that material as causative and directive in itself, that is to say, as holding within itself the plan of its spiritual interpretation. Mechanical learning of facts that can be used toward material ends is then brought to supplant development of human personality in terms of culture, character, and wisdom. Then is life lived from the outside in, instead of from the inside out.

But in music and the arts, which still reveal the necessity and power of imagination and creative thought, the values of a more humanistic education may, perhaps, be best demonstrated; and teachers of music and art should not disregard the opportunity and privilege, and should not remain content to teach their subjects after the methods of mechanical instruction, in a world that so desperately needs spiritual life.

An Experimental Study of Creative Work in Public School Music *

Assumptions underlying creative work

The term 'creative,' as used by educators, has served as a garment of uncertain outlines, dyed with many colors, and made to clothe many diverse forms. Precisely what is meant here by 'creative' and by 'creative work in music' accordingly needs to be defined.

One mark of creative effort, as the Department of Music in Pittsburgh has conceived it, is that it produces something original, distinctive, different. It is in contrast, in this particular, to effort that merely reproduces, and that, when many pupils are concerned, results in products that are uniform, standardized, stereotyped.

Originality or individual distinction in any work, as conceived by the Department of Music, implies mental action that involves imagination (using the word in its etymological significance). Perhaps 'reflection' or 'creative thought' would be preferable terms. Such thought differs

---

* Dr. Will Earhart, Director of Music in the Pittsburgh Public Schools, is responsible for the first section of this article. The experimental study is reported by Dr. Frank M. Gatto, Assistant Director of Research, Pittsburgh Public Schools, The study was conducted by the Department of Curriculum Study and Educational Measurement and Research of the Pittsburgh Public Schools, Dr. David R. Sumstine, Director. It is reprinted by the kind permission of Dr. Ben G. Graham, Superintendent, Pittsburgh Public Schools.

from reproductive memory, in that the new percept or mental acquisition finds contact with the whole mental content in which it was deposited before it is returned in expression. The large mental content, in its turn, has been given its particular form, quality, and extent by the individual interests, predilections, and purposes held by a thinking and willing subject who is like no one else. The product of such integrated thought is therefore certain to be individual, unique.

That the product, though individual and unique, may not equal in worth the available products of masters that, as an alternative to original work, might have been acquired by the pupils, is beside the point. With relation to creative work (which, in any case, we would remind the reader, is far from being the only kind of educational process supported by the Department of Music) education is conceived in terms of depth and pervasiveness of mental function, not in terms of acquisitions literally stored in memory. Memory acquisitions as well as creative thought is, the Department recognizes, needed; but memorizing need not entail conceptual thought, while conceptual thought does presuppose, demand, and stimulate much memory acquisition.

Creative work in music, as in any field, has been assumed, therefore, to awaken and energize thought. Thought, in turn, has been assumed to consist in a turning-over of mental content *in a purposive way,* until a pattern is reached that fulfills the urgent intention. The content, in the present case, is a musical content—is made up of tones, tunes, rhythms, dynamic quantities, that trip, loiter, march, float, rise, droop, shout, or sigh—but the assembling of these into a coherent and satisfying pattern is believed to be not less a matter of mental concentration than is the designing of a building. And since the act is conceived as one that integrates knowledge, imaginative thought, feeling, and purpose, it would follow that such effort would tend to develop general powers of personality and disposition as well as special abilities and appreciative judgments connected with the particular subject. In comparison, at least, an effort toward mere reproductive memory would appear much less vital and promising.

The values hypothesized as described in the foregoing statements are possibly not subject to scientific measurement. The creative work here reported consists, however, not only in improvising melodies, but also in writing them in musical notation upon the staff. This process requires some degree of musical literacy, that is to say, knowledge of musical facts and ability to read and write the language of music. Such knowledge and ability, while not the prime objectives of creative work, are yet necessary objectives in any plan of musical education, and the degree of attainment gained in them by pupils is always a matter of importance. Moreover, they are subject to definite measurement; and since there might be a question as to whether they are not slighted when emphasis is placed on creative work, it was decided to prosecute an experimental study that would at least investigate these factors and would, at the same time, seek light along any other paths that appeared to hold promise of yielding returns. Moreover, since the creative work in music in the Pittsburgh schools had grown to large proportions, and had become almost a fixed feature in the work of all the children, with little to support it except the assumptions and opinions that have herein been reviewed, it was the more imperative that any study that would give promise of even a partial answer as to its validity should be undertaken and pushed promptly to a conclusion.

It remains to be said that under the plan in operation in Pittsburgh no song is improvised or composed by one pupil alone. Instead, some pupil, in a regular class recitation in music, suggests the words and the melody of a phrase, other pupils contribute substitute phrases or additional phrases, and by a long succession of improvisations and choices that may finally involve every pupil in the room the song, as a socialized art project, is finally completed. All then participate in putting the thought in correct musical notation upon the blackboard. Occasionally metrical verses from printed literature are used, but this practice is rare, since the prosodic structure sets a rhythmic pattern, often of a most conventional type, and hence does not leave the pupils entirely free with respect to their melodies. No such suggestion or influence is ever given, however, with respect to the rhythms or tones of the melodies themselves.

The experiment

It is natural that much of the discussion on the liberation of creative effort in school music should remain in the realm of speculation and that the inferences drawn should be based upon the evidence of logic rather than upon empirical proof. Even the extreme experimentalist in education will be forced to concede to those who question the feasibility of an adequate experimental appraisal of music instruction, that his most refined instruments of measurement and his most effective techniques are not sensitized to many vital aspects of learning and that educational outcomes other than information and certain skills tend to elude efforts at measurement. However, when a new or a modified philosophy of education suggests new teaching procedures—new pupil activities—it is always of interest to know what effect these departures may have upon the measurable outcomes of teaching unless, in all strict logic, the new outcomes are absolutely distinct from, and absolutely incompatible with, the measurable outcomes. Unless the latter be the case, objective evidence of some of the results of instruction should be sought. This evidence may, in fact, assist in the clarification of the purely logical inferences. It appears therefore, justifiable to seek, through objective measurements, a partial answer to the problem of creative work in music even in the face of the tenable objection that some of the more significant aspects of creative work are, for the present, beyond measurement.

This study is an attempt to determine the relative effectiveness of creative pupil activities as compared to conventional pupil activities in the work of fifth grade music classes when the measurement of effectiveness is in terms of certain standardized music tests and certain appraisals by competent critics of public school music. This investigation is of experimental nature and involves the establishment of the controls described below. The experiment is of the equated groups type and, as such, presented the alternative plans of using groups with different teachers or groups assigned to the same instructor. It was determined to eliminate the teacher variable by the selection of both the control and the experimental group from classes under the same teacher. It would have been possible to select teachers judged to be equal in ability by the use of devices and procedures currently utilized to measure teacher ability, but the uncertain character of such measurements suggested, as preferable, the use of one teacher for both groups. In fact, the writers are skeptical of classroom experimentation where the only precaution taken to avoid the teacher variable lies in the assumed equality of different teachers supported by rating scale estimates.

However, the selection of one teacher does not, necessarily, remove the teacher variable unless care is exercised in choosing a teacher without bias toward either of the elements of comparison. Great caution must be exercised lest even a dimly conceived prejudice may weight results in a given direction. The best control possible would seem to rest in (a) the assignment of classes to teachers not conscious of bias and (b) the prescription of classroom activities, materials, etc., to prevent any possible intrusion of bias. It was felt by the director of music that the teacher chosen met the essential qualifications. An additional safeguard in the maintenance of the proper conditions for experimentation was the assignment of a supervisor who kept in constant and intimate touch with the work done in the classroom.

Two classes in grade 5A, of the Holmes School, were used in the study. This naturally restricted the number of pupils far more than was acceptable to the writers. However, the experiment was intended to yield tentative rather than final evidence. It was felt, furthermore, that controls would be more easily maintained and that the experiences incident to this study might prove useful in the prosecution of similar studies on a large scale if such were later deemed feasible and desirable.

The experimental and the control class contained 35 pupils each. However, in pairing, the number was reduced to 26 in each group. The equating was based upon two factors: (a) scores on the Kwalwasser-Dykema Music Tests and (b) class attendance. The obvious importance of the latter factor requires no comment; a brief description of the music tests may, however, be pertinent and may prove of interest to any reader who is not familiar with them. The tests are for the measurement of musical capacity although musical training is called into play. The administration of the ten tests involves the use of phonograph records. The responses are entered upon a test blank. The first test measures "Tonal Memory." It contains twenty-five pairs of musical patterns of varying difficulty. The pupil records whether the two patterns constituting each pair appear to be the same or different. The second test, on "Quality Discrimination," tests the recognition of similarity or difference in tone quality. The third test measures "Intensity Discrimination." It contains, like the second, thirty items. The test calls into play the ability to distinguish the intensity of sounds. The fourth test deals with "Tonal Movement." It contains thirty items and requires the pupil to determine how the incomplete musical patterns presented are best completed. The fifth test is designated as one on "Time Discrimination." In the responses to its twenty items the pupil indicates whether notes presented together are of equal length or whether they differ. The sixth test measures "Rhythm Discrimination." This test has twenty-five items. Pupils are required to indicate whether rhythms given together are the same or different. The seventh test is on "Pitch Discrimination." Its forty items require pupils to indicate whether the pitch of tones given is the same or different. The eighth test, on "Melodic Taste," requires twenty responses in which pupils indicate the preferred melodies between the pairs presented. The ninth test is on "Pitch Imagery." It has twenty-five items presented on the test blank. The pupil is to indicate whether items played on the phonograph record are similar to or different from the items printed on the test sheet. The tenth test, "Rhythm Imagery" has twenty-five items and is given in a manner similar to the administration of the preceding test. Pupils are to indicate whether items played on the phonograph are the same as or different from those printed on the test sheet.

The similarity of the two groups in respect to test scores is shown in Table I. It would appear that the 26 pairs of

TABLE I

MEANS AND STANDARD DEVIATIONS ON KWALWASSER-DYKEMA
MUSIC TEST SCORES FOR EXPERIMENTAL AND CONTROL GROUPS

Group	Number of Cases	Mean	S.D.
Experimental	26	167.50	9.81
Control	26	167.12	8.76

pupils remaining after the equating of groups are strikingly similar in regard to the capacities measured by the test used. In respect to attendance, a very striking similarity is shown in Table II. The groups are, therefore, equated in terms of

TABLE II

MEANS AND STANDARD DEVIATIONS OF THE NUMBER OF CLASS
PERIODS ATTENDED BY PUPILS OF CONTROL AND
EXPERIMENTAL GROUPS

Group	Number of Cases	Mean	S.D.
Experimental	26	53.0	3.28
Control	26	52.6	2.88

school grade, test results, and classroom attendance during the period of this study. The selection of pupils was made by the pairing of a pupil in one group with a pupil in the other group identical, or nearly so, in respect to the factors mentioned.

The average attendance of the two groups was 93 per cent of the total time the experiment was in progress. Classes met three times per week from February 6 to June 12 or a total of 57 periods during the course of the study.

The instructional material used by both groups and the teaching procedures were the same in all respects except that the experimental group spent the last fifteen minutes of each period in the composition and the writing of original songs. Inasmuch as the length of the class period was 40 minutes, it is clear that the group doing creative work spent about 38 per cent of its time in such activities. The control group spent the entire time with printed instructional material which occupied only 25 of the 40 minutes in the case of the other group.

Six original songs constituted the production of the creative activities of the experimental class. They are presented here in the belief that they may be of interest to certain readers. It should be explained, to those who are prone to consider these productions on their own musical merits and as apart from the circumstances of their creation, that these songs represent the first effort at original work by the pupil composers, that the list represents all the songs written and hence is not selective, and that every note composed was written in notation by the pupils themselves.

THE SNOW

Soft - ly, soft - ly the snow comes in win - ter time; It comes down slow - ly. All the night it falls, it spreads a blan - ket o - ver the town.

A JOLLY DAY

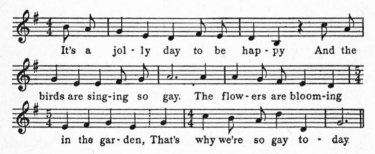

It's a jol - ly day to be hap - py And the birds are sing - ing so gay. The flow - ers are bloom - ing in the gar - den, That's why we're so gay to - day.

THE SUN

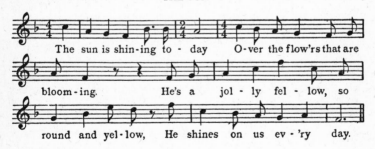

The sun is shin - ing to - day O - ver the flow'rs that are bloom - ing. He's a jol - ly fel - low, so round and yel - low, He shines on us ev - 'ry day.

THE RAIN

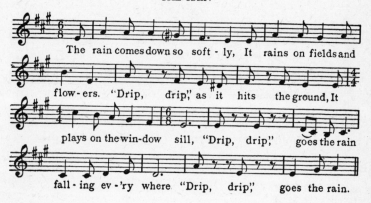

GRANDFATHER'S CLOCK

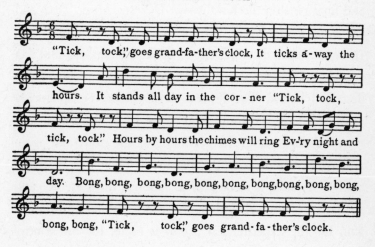

SAILING

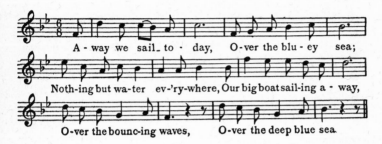

A - way we sail_ to - day, O - ver the blu - ey sea;

Noth-ing but wa-ter ev-'ry-where, Our big boat sail-ing a - way,

O - ver the bounc-ing waves, O - ver the deep blue sea.

Results

The results of the study were measured on the following basis: (a) gains, or differences between scores on initial and final tests on the Kwalwasser-Dykema Music Tests and the Kwalwasser-Ruch Test of Musical Accomplishment; (b) scores on a dictation test to be later described; and (c) appraisals, by competent critics, of musical performances described below. The Kwalwasser-Dykema Tests, already described, gave the results shown in Table III. These tests were administered at the beginning of the study and again at its termination and the means of Table III represent gains. The table is to be read as follows: there are 26 cases in the experimental and in the control group; the mean gain for the experimental group is 6.538, for the control

TABLE III

RESULTS ON KWALWASSER-DYKEMA MUSIC TESTS FOR EXPERIMENTAL
AND CONTROL GROUPS

Group	N	Mean	SD Dis.	SD Mean	Diff. Means	SD Diff.	Ratio D–SD Diff.	Chances in 100 of True Difference Greater than 0
Experimental ...	26	6.538	7.732	1.52				
					.923	2.263	.41	65
Control	26	5.615	7.976	1.56				

group, 5.615; the standard deviation of the distribution
for the experimental group is 7.732, for the control group,
7.976; the standard error of the difference (the formula
taking cognizance of the factor of correlation was used)
is 2.263 which makes the ratio of the difference to its
standard error equal to .41 thus indicating that there are
65 chances in 100 of a true difference greater than zero.

The results on the Kwalwasser-Ruch Test of Musical
Accomplishment are given in Table IV. Table IV is read in
the same manner as Table III. The test, which is "designed
to measure the achievement of pupils in the typical public
school music course in the elementary and high school
grades," contains the following divisions: (1) Knowledge

TABLE IV

RESULTS ON KWALWASSER-RUCH TEST OF MUSICAL ACCOMPLISHMENT
FOR EXPERIMENTAL AND CONTROL GROUPS

Group	N	Mean	SD Dis.	SD Mean	Diff. Means	SD Diff.	Ratio D–SD Diff.	Chances in 100 of True Difference Greater than 0
Experimental	26	35.385	17.984	3.53				
					12.116	4.723	2.57	99
Control.....	26	23.269	13.351	2.62				

of Musical Symbols and Terms, (2) Recognition of Syllable Names, (3) Detection of Pitch Errors in a Familiar Melody, (4) Detection of Time Errors in a Familiar Melody, (5) Recognition of Pitch Names, (6) Knowledge of Time Signatures, (7) Knowledge of Key Signatures, (8) Knowledge of Note Values, (9) Knowledge of Rest Values, and (10) Recognition of Familiar Melodies from Notation. It will be noted that the experimental group again shows an advantage over the control group and that, in the case of the last test mentioned, the reliability of the difference is considerably greater than it was on the first test. This would seem natural, inasmuch as the Kwalwasser-Dykema Test purports to measure musical capacity and would, therefore, give results which vary less as the result of learning than would be the case with musical accomplishment. However, it is noteworthy that the results from both tests favor the experimental group.

A third test to measure the differences between the two groups was an unstandardized test in written musical dictation. Since this test was constructed specifically for this experiment and is not elsewhere available, it is reproduced on page 236. The test contains three melodies presented in the order given. Pupils were allowed ten minutes to write each one and the work on one melody was completed before the presentation of the one following. The teacher announced the key of a melody before dictating it. The procedure of administering the test involved the singing of each melody by the teacher to the neutral syllable "la." After the teacher sang the melody three times, it was imitated by the pupils. Then, in the case of the first two

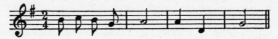

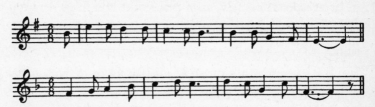

melodies, the melody was played by the teacher upon the piano after asking pupils to listen attentively and to think of the syllables applying to the tones. The next step, with the first and second melodies, was for the pupils to sing each melody by syllables. Then each melody was sung by the pupils again following the suggestion of the teacher that on this singing accents be located and the bars and kind of measure represented be visualized. Each melody was then written on the music paper provided. The third melody was presented in a similar manner with the exception of the fact that in no step of the procedure was the melody sung by syllables. The marking of the papers was done on the basis of the following directions:

(a) Each key-signature is reckoned as *one* symbol and is marked wrong if not wholly right.

(b) Each measure-signature is similarly reckoned as *one* symbol and is marked wrong if not wholly right.

(c) Each measure-bar is a symbol. A bar out of place is

marked wrong; omission of a bar is an error; but a bar transposed, so that it is out of place, and is also missing from its proper place, constitutes only one error.

(d) Each note is a symbol. While a note may be in error in two respects; namely, as to placement and as to denomination, each note will be marked wrong unless it is *wholly* right.

(e) Each rest is a symbol. If misplaced, or of wrong denomination, either or both, it is marked wrong.

TABLE V

RESULTS ON DICTATION TEST FOR EXPERIMENTAL AND CONTROL GROUPS

Group	N	Mean	SD Dis	SD Means	Diff. Means	SD Diff.	Ratio D–SD Diff.	Chances in 100 of True Difference Greater than 0
Experimental	26	30.615	13.975	2.74				
					10.769	3.512	3.066	100
Control.....	26	19.846	9.875	1.94				

The results of the Dictation Test are given in Table V. This table again shows the ascendancy of the experimental group. In this case the ratio of the difference to its standard error is more than sufficient to indicate the complete reliability of the difference.

As a further appraisal of the status of the two groups, four music critics, held by the director of the music department as competent to judge the musical performance of public school pupils, evaluated the singing of the two classes in terms of certain criteria, evolved by the director, and applied to two musical performances described below.

In the first performance, which will be referred to as *Event Number 1,* the judges, unknown to either group and unaware of the identity of either group as the experimental or control class, judged the singing of six songs [1] on the basis of the criteria given in Table VI. As indicated in the table, each song might receive a maximum of ten points on the second, third, and fourth criteria. The maximum score on the first criterion was sixty points. The scores given in the table represent, with the obvious exception of the first criterion, the sum of the points allotted by each judge to all six songs on each criterion. The songs used were, specifically:

(a) Dialogue—At the Window (Unison)
(b) Swallows (Unison)
(c) Mother (Unison)
(d) Lady Willow (Two Parts)
(e) Colonial Maid (Two Parts)
(f) Pastorale (Two Parts)

The songs were taken from the *Music Education Series:* the second from *Intermediate Music;* the other, from *Two-Part Music.* The teacher assembled the classes in turn and conducted each through a "warming-up" song. Then she stated that the pupils were to sing some songs to her as a "concert." She announced the pages and titles of songs but did not direct the singing. A supervisor accompanied all songs at the piano but did not *lead* from the piano.

[1] These were recently learned repertory songs.

TABLE VI

TOTAL NUMBER OF POINTS ALLOTTED BY EACH OF FOUR CRITICS TO THE EXPERIMENTAL AND THE CONTROL GROUPS ON EVENT NUMBER I

Criteria	Experimental Group Judges					Control Group Judges				
	1	2	3	4	Total	1	2	3	4	Total
1. Degree of enthusiasm with which the pupils appear to greet the prospect of the music lesson or exercise, before the lesson has begun. Maximum 60 points	55	45	50	50	200	45	45	40	40	170
2. Degree of whole-souled absorption or devotion to music, as apparent in attitudes while singing familiar songs not directed by the teacher. Maximum 10 points on each song.	47	49	46	43	185	41	47	46	50	184
3. Degree of sensitivity to tonal features as shown in distaste for bad tone quality, inaccuracies in pitch, errors in rhythm (or care for the opposites of these), while singing familiar songs not directed by the teacher. Maximum 10 points on each song.	40	48	46	41	175	35	41	43	40	159
4. Degree of aesthetic feeling as revealed in sensitive dynamic shadings, variety in voice qualities and delivery, rhythmic freedom, while singing familiar songs not directed by the teacher. Maximum 10 points on each song.	42	51	44	43	180	31	40	47	50	168
TOTAL	184	193	186	177	740	152	173	176	180	681

It will be noted that in all the criteria the experimental group received higher ratings and that the total number of points allotted this group exceed by about nine per cent the points allotted the performance of the control group. Of course, it may readily be objected that judgments arrived at by the critics are purely subjective. But in refutation may be urged the care taken to prevent bias, the fact that three of the four judges rated the total performance of the experimental group as superior, and the consistency with which ratings follow the trend indicated by the objective tests used in this study.

In *Event Number 2,* the critics passed judgment on the singing, at sight, of the song, "Swallows," by the two groups.[1] Neither group previously had either heard the song or had seen its notation. Each group sang the song three times, using the *so-fa* syllables on the first two attempts and the words of the first stanza on the third attempt. At the outset, the teacher played the F-major chord, beyond which no help or slightest prompting of any kind with respect to any factors of tempo, rhythm, pitch, or syllable names was given the pupils. The ratings given by each judge for the three trials are shown in Table VII. In this last performance of the classes used in the study, the experimental group receives a rating exceeding by about 21 per cent the rating of the control group. The total ratings of the four judges are consistently in favor of the experimental group. Objections which may be made to them would appear to be the same as in the case of the data of Table VI. Perhaps the most significant point which may be stressed is that in all the appraisals attempted in this study, the experimental group is superior.

---

[1] This song "Swallows" is a wholly different song from that used in the preceding test which bore the same title. It is from a different book, and one which the pupils had not seen.

TABLE VII

TOTAL NUMBER OF POINTS ALLOTTED BY EACH OF FOUR CRITICS TO THE EXPERI-
MENTAL AND CONTROL GROUPS ON EVENT NUMBER 2

Criteria	Experimental Group Judges					Control Group Judges				
	1	2	3	4	Total	1	2	3	4	Total
1. Ability to conceive and execute musically the RHYTHMIC thought. Maximum, each trial, 10 points.	18	24	23	28	93	13	22	22	22	79
2. Ability to conceive and execute musically the MELODIC thought. Maximum, each trial, 10 points.	21	22	20	18	81	16	15	17	19	67
3. Ability to grasp and interpret the ARTISTIC conception. Maximum, each trial, 10 points.	15	21	14	15	65	11	9	17	15	52
TOTAL	54	67	57	61	239	40	46	56	56	198

Summary and conclusions

The experimental study described attempted to determine the relative effectiveness of creative pupil activities as compared with conventional pupil activities in the work of fifth grade music classes, basing the comparison on certain standardized music tests and certain appraisals by critics of elementary school music. The study is of the equated-groups type, the pairing of pupils being effected on the basis of grade, results on the Kwalwasser-Dykema music tests, and attendance during the course of the study. The teacher variable was eliminated by placing both the experimental and the control group in charge of the same teacher. The experiment occupied a period of 19 weeks with classes meeting for three forty minute periods each week. The instructional materials and procedures were the same for both groups, except that the experimental group spent fifteen minutes of each period in the composition and writing of original songs. The results were measured on (a) gains on the Kwalwasser-Dykema Music Tests; (b) gains on the Kwalwasser-Ruch Tests of Musical Accomplishment; (c) scores on a dictation test administered at the end of the study; and (d) the rating of two performances of the groups by four critics held competent to judge public school music. The results of the tests and the judges' appraisals consistently attributed superiority to the experimental group.

Unfortunately, the number of cases is somewhat small for full reliance upon the outcomes. However, within the limits of the conditions described, the comparisons here made between creative pupil activities and conventional pupil activities in the work of fifth grade music classes, would appear to indicate the superiority of the former.

—WILL EARHART
Director of Music

—FRANK M. GATTO
Assistant Director of Research

BIBLIOGRAPHY

The scope of this book is so comprehensive that a thorough treatment of all the subjects discussed in it was impossible unless the book were unduly extended. Such extension would moreover have destroyed its right proportions by giving too much space to general philosophical and aesthetic topics. On the other hand, the book may find use as a textbook in the hands of young college students or graduates, and these may lack the background of reading in philosophy and aesthetics that would give the brief discussions herein any adequate significance. Such students will need to supplement this volume by additional readings in the fields mentioned. The books that could be recommended for this purpose are innumerable, but the short list following, with specific chapters cited, may be offered as representative, and as a minimum requirement. Citations in the text will suggest other readings; and any instructor who uses the book as a text will doubtless wish to make substitutions and additions, in these departments, out of his own knowledge. In connection with *Part Three* and *Part Four* of the book no readings are specified, since current literature and texts abound, and are brought to the attention of every student who prepares to enter the music education field. The General List appended, may, however, offer suggestions.

For Supplementary Reading

In connection with PART ONE, "A Philosophical Basis."

BERGSON, HENRI: *Mind-Energy* (Henry Holt and Company) (Translation, H. Wildon Carr), Chapters I, II, III, and VII.

DEWEY, JOHN: *Reconstruction in Philosophy* (Henry Holt and Company), Chapters I-V, inclusive.

FOX, CHARLES: *The Mind and Its Body* (Harcourt, Brace and Company), Chapters II, XI, XII.

HALDANE, J. S.: *Materialism* (Harper and Bros.), Chapters II, III, VI, VIII.

In connection with PART Two, "An Aesthetic Basis."

GURNEY, EDMUND: *The Power of Sound* (Smith, Elder and Company, London), Chapter XIV.

LEE, VERNON: *The Beautiful* (Cambridge University Press), Chapters I-V, inclusive.

PRALL, D. W.: *Æsthetic Judgment* (Thomas Y. Crowell Company), Chapters I-VI, inclusive.

SANTAYANA, GEORGE: *The Sense of Beauty* (Charles Scribner's Sons), pp. 52-104.

SCHOEN, MAX: *Art and Beauty* (The Macmillan Company), Chapter VI.

GENERAL LIST

In addition to the unspecified portions of the books named in the foregoing list, which are recommended for general reading, the books following have value, either because they strengthen the background of thought, enrich and vary its content, or extend its practical applications. All, however, are not (as, indeed, was the case with some of the books in the preceding list) in accord at every point with the beliefs upheld in this volume. Nevertheless—or perhaps for that very reason—they deserve to be read; for at least they carry the reader to the terrain in which truth must be sought; and at that point every searcher helps all the others.

In case only portions of a book named are closely relevant to our discussion, those portions (provided they are compartmentalized and can be separated from the remainder) are specifically recommended. Such specification does not mean, however, that other parts of those books are to be avoided.

BELL, CLIVE: *Art* (Frederick A. Stokes Company), Parts I, II, and V.

BERGSON, HENRI: *Creative Evolution* (translated by Arthur Mitchell) (Henry Holt and Company), Chapters II and III.

BIRGE, EDWARD BAILEY: *History of Public School Music in the United States* (Oliver Ditson Company).

CABOT, RICHARD C.: *What Men Live By* (Houghton Mifflin Company), Chapters XII and XXVIII, in particular.

DEWEY, JOHN: *How We Think* (D. C. Heath and Company).

FARNSWORTH, CHARLES HUBERT: *Education through Music* (American Book Company), all, but especially Chapters I-V, inclusive, and XIX.

FITE, WARNER: *Individualism* (Longmans, Green and Co.), Lecture II, in particular.

—— *The Living Mind* (The Dial Press).

GEHRKENS, KARL WILSON: *Music in the Grade Schools* (C. C. Birchard & Co.).

GENTILE, GIOVANNI: *The Reform of Education* (Translated by Dino Bigongiari) (Harcourt, Brace and Company).

HENDERSON, C. HANFORD: *Education and the Larger Life* (Houghton Mifflin Company).

—— *What Is It To Be Educated* (Houghton Mifflin Company).

HENDERSON, ERNEST NORTON: *A Textbook in the Principles of Education* (The Macmillan Company), especially Chapters VIII and XI.

JUNG, C. G.: *Modern Man in Search of a Soul* (Harcourt, Brace and Company), Chapter IX especially.

KWALWASSER, JACOB: *Problems in Public School Music* (M. Witmark and Sons).

MEARNS, HUGHES: *Creative Power* (Doubleday, Doran & Company, Inc.).

—— *Creative Youth* (Doubleday, Page & Company).

MORRIS, WILLIAM: *Signs of Change* (Longmans, Green and Co.), especially the essay, "The Aims of Art."

MURSELL, JAMES L.: *Human Values in Music Education* (Silver, Burdett and Company).

—— *Principles of Musical Education* (The Macmillan Company).

MURSELL, JAMES L., and GLENN MABELLE: *The Psychology of School Music Teaching* (Silver, Burdett and Company).

PUFFER, ETHEL: *The Psychology of Beauty* (Houghton Mifflin Company).

REID, LOUIS ARNAUD: *A Study in Aesthetics* (The Macmillan Company), Chapters I-V especially.

SCHOPENHAUER, ARTHUR: *The World as Will and Idea*, 3 vols.; various parts; search *Index* for subjects, as "Art," "Consciousness,"

"Idea," "Music," etc. (Translated by R. B. Haldane and J. Kemp) (Kegan Paul, Trench, Trübner & Co., Ltd., London).

SEASHORE, CARL EMIL: *The Psychology of Musical Talent* (Silver, Burdett and Company).

SHEEN, FULTON J.: *Old Errors and New Labels;* especially "Cosmic Intimidation," "The Wax Nose of Scientific Authority," "The Philosophy of Medieval Art," etc. (The Century Co.).

STANTON, HAZEL M., and KOERTH, WILHELMINE: *Musical Capacity Measures of Children Repeated after Musical Training* (The University, Iowa City, Iowa).

STREETER, BURNETT HILLMAN: *Reality* (The Macmillan Company), Chapters I and IV.

WAGNER, RICHARD: *Opera and Drama* (Translated by William Ashton Ellis) (Kegan Paul, Trench, Trübner & Co., Ltd., London), First Part.

INDEX

Absolute pitch: a physical rather than a musical concern, 129.

Aesthetic fusion: in programmatic music, 79; in opera, 80.

Aesthetic response: as a mode, 50; as satisfaction in contemplation, 53; depth and amplitude, 56 et seq.; validity, 59; to great music, 82-4; in the child, 90; value of, 91.

Art: defined by Balzac, 54; as representing satisfying relationships between things outside ourselves, 53-5; Santayana on art, 65 et seq.

Attention: as perceptive or as intuitive, 51-2, 89.

Auditory imagery: as developed by retention, 114; devices for developing it, 114-5; the basis of musical power, 120; as used creatively by the mind, 204, 209-10; such musical endowment widely held, 211; as the material for musical thought, 215.

Bacon: 1, 24; his philosophy, 1, 13.

Bell, Clive: on "human emotion" from music, 73-4; defines art, 76.

Bergson: 1; on rationalistic thought, 2; on science, 4; on rational intellect, 5; on method of science, 21; on realism, 36; on perception, 37; on mind and brain, 42, 43, 44; on aesthetic intuition, 51; on undivided act of mind, 139; on memory, object, and image, 205.

Brain: brain and mind, 42-3.

Cabot, Richard: on aesthetic response as highly vitalized, 57-8.

Chambers, Will Grant: on action of the mind in education, 143.

Chorus (see also Vocal Music): characteristics of music produced, in comparison with orchestra, 155-8; influence upon members, as compared with orchestra, 187-8.

Claxton, P. P.: on feeling vs. thought, 57.

Consciousness: as Reality, 33-4; as not defined in the physical, 37-8.

Cox, Kenyon: on craftsman and artist, 120.

Creative Education (see also Education): mental activity as creative, 192-3; contrasted with mechanical learning, 193-4; the point of view of creative education defined, 195-6; as developmental of individuality, 196-7; values lost in mechanical learning, 197-8; general features, 198-9; dangers and their avoidance, 199-201; applied to music, with reference to auditory imagery and memory, 204-6; with respect to reproductive memory for knowledge, and auditory imagery for creative use, 206-7; prevalence of creative musical power among persons, 211; improvisation as thought, 211-13; musical thought identical with all thought, 214-15; value to the character of the learner, 215-16; value as music education, 217-18; all thought as creative, and as distinct from mechanical learning, 218-19; an experimental study of creative education in music, 221-42.

Descartes: 1.

Design in music: see "Form in music."

Determinism: 7.

247